Recovery from Narcissistic Abuse, Gaslighting, Codependency, Trauma Bond & Complex PTSD

The Ultimate Guide to Overcoming Toxic and Unhealthy Relationships, Emotional Abuse & Break Free of Trauma Bonds

by

ANNA WILEY

Table of Contents

Introduction

Do you still feel attached to someone who caused you physical, mental, or emotional harm?

Have you suffered abuse from this person, yet you can't seem to let go of them or stop thinking about them?

If you've answered yes to these questions, this may be due to trauma bonding. Trauma bonding occurs when someone who has been abused forms an unhealthy attachment to their abuser. This kind of connection often happens in relationships over a period of time, and it develops through a repeated cycle of abuse. One specific and well-known type of trauma bond is Stockholm Syndrome, which refers to a connection formed between those in captivity and their captors.

The "love" one feels in a trauma bond is often confused for real love, because in both situations, the feelings are extremely intense. However, real and honest love would never harm you or cause pain. A trauma bond aims to do just that, and it will keep you trapped in the cycle of abuse. This can cause confusion and even cognitive dissonance, in which you may notice your beliefs and thoughts constantly changing and shifting. Abuse alone creates a faulty memory and trouble focusing, and when it becomes a trauma bond, it can keep you trapped in this state of psychological inconsistency and reliance on your abuser.

You may be wondering, *How do I know for sure if I'm in a trauma-bonded relationship?* Well, do you often cover for the abuser? Are you reluctant to leave your bad situation? Have you distanced yourself from family or friends who are trying to help you? All of these signs will be discussed and analyzed in depth later in the book so you can know for sure where you stand.

Leaving *any* relationship is difficult, but it is especially hard to leave abusive and toxic relationships that have formed a trauma bond. Trauma bonding is dangerous for mental and emotional health. If you have been experiencing its symptoms, then you know how cyclical and overwhelming it becomes. We will talk about the ways you can break free from this bond. This will not happen immediately. These bonds take time to form, and they take time to break, as well. However, once you are armed with an awareness of exactly what you are dealing with and how it affects your thoughts, feelings, and behaviors, you can begin to take back control of your life, stop the cycle of abuse, and break free from this toxic bond for good.

| Part 1 | Understanding the Basics

Section 1: What is Trauma Bonding?

Trauma bonding is an intimidating and confusing term. One might wonder, how do bonds form through trauma? Well, the human psyche is very interesting; we actually cope with abuse and suffering by attaching ourselves to those around us. The term "trauma bonding" refers to the psychological response our body and mind have to abuse. It specifically happens when the mistreated person forms an unhealthy attachment to the abuser (Johnson and Zoppi 2020). They find a way to cope with the abusive situation by attaching themselves to the abusive person.

We all form natural attachments to each other. But in toxic and abusive relationships, these attachments are heightened because of the intense feelings that cause confusion. Most abusive relationships do not *begin* this way. It starts slowly, and there may be some red flags, but they are usually things you can brush off. Generally, there is a great deal of passion, love, and intimacy at the beginning of the relationship, which forms an attachment. You may feel that you have found your soulmate, or that you've "never felt this way before." Slowly, things will start changing. Then, when the abuse starts, you are shocked and left wondering where you went wrong. You may be confused and unable to pinpoint exactly where things started changing because it all started so slowly.

As an abuser tries to keep you trapped, manipulation and other psychological games come to play. For example, if your partner suddenly begins yelling, berating you, and swearing like they never have before, you will obviously have feelings of sadness, hurt, and maybe even some anger yourself. However, on the other hand, your partner may simply chalk their behavior up to a bad day. They may say dismissive things like "I let my anger get the best of me and it won't happen again," or "I only got so mad because you said..."

This is a common form of manipulation known as **gaslighting**. Gaslighting is used by many abusers as a way to change the narrative and attempt to alter the victim's reality into something that will shift blame away from the abuser. Those who are being gaslighted often feel similar to those who are in the grips of a trauma bond. They have feelings of confusion and doubt, and they may regularly experience cognitive dissonance. While it may seem like this would push any person away, in a trauma bond, this does just the opposite. This is because the person being gaslighted is not *always* being gaslighted; they may feel that their partner is not bad *all* the time, and simply believe their behavior was only a mistake. However, as the gaslighting becomes more extreme, the trauma bond becomes stronger as well. If the abuser is effective in their use of gaslighting, the victim will begin to filter their entire understanding of reality through the abuser. Because they are regularly told that they cannot trust their perception of reality, they will trust their *abuser's* perceptions of events, placing them deeper in their hold.

The ways in which these toxic people can abuse you vary widely. They may inflict mental, emotional, or even physical abuse. In some cases, betrayal plays a large part, as well. While it may seem that this would create separation rather than a bond, it can actually strengthen the unhealthy attachment. This kind of **betrayal trauma** can occur when the abuser is someone you depend on for certain needs. You may choose to accept their betrayal to continue receiving what they provide for you, sacrificing emotional safety, love, etc. in order to have a place to live or enough money to survive.

In addition to this, you may even begin making excuses and accepting future betrayal behavior from this same person in an attempt to reason with yourself for staying. This is explained by betrayal trauma theory which started as a psychological concept in 1991; we will discuss this further in the following sections.

Summary

- Trauma bonding occurs when someone forms an unhealthy attachment to their abuser.
- The feelings associated with real love and the symptoms of trauma bonding are often confused due to their comparable intensity.
- Psychological tactics such as gaslighting are used to manipulate victims and trap them in toxic and abusive relationships.

In the next section, you will learn how the betrayal trauma theory began and what its importance is to toxic connections.

Section 2: Betrayal Trauma Theory

Betrayal trauma theory was founded in 1991 by psychologist Dr. Jennifer Freyd. She described the theory as a situation in which the betrayed individual continues to maintain a relationship with the betrayer out of necessity. This can cause lasting trauma and psychological dependence, especially if the dependent individual is a child. As stated in the previous sections, many people would leave a relationship or situation in which betrayal happened. However, when they are left with no other option, they may stay and form this unhealthy bond. Children in this situation may be unable to process or fully understand what has happened.

Early childhood is a critical time for emotional and mental growth. It's when we are first recognizing our emotions, exploring how we relate to the world, and understanding the way others perceive us. If our caregivers are abusive to us physically or emotionally, it can damage the way we relate to others around us and the image we hold about ourselves. When we don't have a healthy relationship with our caregivers, it damages the attachment that we form with them. **Attachment theory** states that a child's early relationships, primarily with parents or other caregivers, can impact their relationships later on in life. A caregiver is supposed to foster a healthy and safe environment for their child. Without this, a child will not form a strong attachment to their caregiver, and will never learn the proper way to do so. This can go on to cause *many* symptoms, detailed below, and it will also affect their ability to form healthy social and romantic relationships in the future.

Because children are still in the formative stages of life, they may experience **dissociation** from the situation in order to cope with the overwhelming emotions associated with abuse. Dissociation refers to the brain "zoning out" or completely detaching from a situation. It's a way to avoid processing emotions instead of facing them head-on. Because it functions to help the abused party ignore their abuse and trauma, it helps them cope in the short-term but strengthens their trauma bond to their abuser in the long term.

Betrayal trauma theory originally only pertained to the relationship between a parent and a child, but it has been shown that it connects to other relationships as well. For example, it could also be present in a romantic relationship where one partner depends on another for finances. While we don't necessarily depend on our romantic partners later in life to provide us with necessities such as food or clothing that our early caregivers must provide us with, we *do* depend on them for love, compassion, and understanding. If these needs are not met, but we still depend on them for other things, such as a home or finances, then we may need to sacrifice our need for compassion or love in order to meet these other, more basic needs.

Often, betrayal in romantic relationships comes in the form of cheating or infidelity. This can be traumatic because when we enter into a relationship with someone, we are trusting them with not only our physical body but our emotional well-being as well. You may not need your partner in order to survive, but you may be hesitant to leave for a variety of reasons. For example, you may have children with your partner, or you may depend on them for finances, family, friends, etc.

However, the only way to deal with the betrayal is to acknowledge it. This is difficult, and it can be impossible for children who are too young to do so. As an adult, though, it's important to recognize these symptoms. Betrayal is a dangerous part of trauma bonding; it is one of the main aspects that can add to an already toxic situation. When we experience betrayal, be it from a parent, romantic partner, or someone else, it can affect our physical, emotional, and mental health. Any abused party will experience and process their trauma uniquely, but there are some common symptoms for both childhood and relationship betrayal:

Symptoms of Betrayal	
Childhood Abuse Betrayal	**Romantic Abuse Betrayal**
Mental health problems, such as anxiety and/or depression	Low self-esteem, paranoia, and/or inability to trust in others
Unexplained physical illnesses	Unexplained physical symptoms
Addictions and/or eating disorders	Feelings of numbness
Nightmares	Dwelling on the relationship
Difficulty processing and expressing emotions	Guilt and shame

Throughout this book, we will talk about more symptoms of trauma bonds, ways you can cultivate awareness of its symptoms, and the proven ways to break them.

Summary

- Betrayal theory originally only was recognized in the relationship between a child and caregiver but was found to be relevant in romantic and social relationships as well

- Symptoms of betrayal trauma in childhood & romantic partnerships.

- The only way to break the betrayal bond is through a recognition of the reality of the situation.

In the next section, you will learn what causes trauma bonding and when it happens.

Section 3: When Does Trauma Bonding Happen?

It may be difficult to identify when trauma bonding takes place. While there may not be one instance that you can point to and identify as the beginning of it all, there are ways to pinpoint certain causes and overarching scenarios that are common in many trauma-bonded relationships. It's good to be aware of when trauma bonding can happen, because we may be able to recognize its formation before it takes full effect over our relationship.

A trauma bond can form in any of the following situations:

- **Domestic or child abuse.** This toxic environment is damaging to both the psyche and physical body of the abused party in certain situations. It can be hard to see outside of an abusive situation, especially if your abuser is someone who is supposed to love and care for you, like a parent.
- **Incest.** Sexual relations between people who are closely related, especially when these relations are nonconsensual, creates confusion and a misconstrued concept of what makes a healthy relationship.
- **Kidnapping or human trafficking.** In these situations, a specific type of trauma bond can form called Stockholm Syndrome
- **Cults.** Cults and isolated situations create an alternate reality for the abused party. When victims are cut off from the rest of the world and their only frame of reference is their cult, it can be nearly impossible to decipher between what is normal behavior and what is abusive.

In order for a trauma bond to develop, the following conditions need to be met:

- **Threat from the abuser.** Whether this threat is real or perceived is irrelevant. Even if the threat is only perceived, it will trigger the same chemical response in the body needed to form a trauma bond. The abuser may verbally threaten their victim, they may have physically harmed the victim in the past, or they may just be a naturally angry person that rages, creating the sense that there always could be danger.
- **Abuse followed by kindness.** The abuser is not *always* abusive and needs to keep their victim in a state of confusion, wondering why one minute they are kind

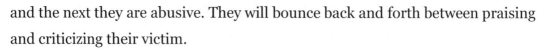

and the next they are abusive. They will bounce back and forth between praising and criticizing their victim.

- **Isolation.** In order for the bond to be strong, the victim has to be cut off from others who may recognize that the attachment between the abuser and the victim is unhealthy. These people could get in the way of the abuser hurting the victim, and therefore they cannot be present in the relationship on a regular basis.

- **Inability to escape.** This can also be perceived or real, but the victim must *feel* that they cannot escape, keeping them trapped in this unhealthy attachment.

It's important to note that the abuse does not have to be physical for a trauma bond to form. Psychological and emotional abuse are equally as damaging and often accompany physical abuse.

So, we know now that trauma bonding happens in abusive and toxic relationships. However, if you are in one of these dangerous situations, you may still be struggling to understand why this has happened to your relationship. Let's look at a few possibilities:

1. **Attachment.** Humans are social creatures and we are constantly forming attachments. We need positive interaction to survive. These attachments can form positive and healthy relationships initially, and then quickly turn sour. If one of your main social attachments is also your abuser, you may not want to leave them out of fear of being alone. It can be a comfort to stay in a relationship that is familiar, even if the other person is harmful to you. When we are desperate to form an attachment, then we may fall prey to an abuser, making us vulnerable to the formation of a trauma bond. Many abusers look for people who only want to be loved. This is where they will employ techniques to make you feel loved and secure in order to lure you in before showing their true colors to you.

2. **Cyclical Nature.** Many people who have never experienced abuse do not understand why people stay in relationships that cause damage to their emotional and/or physical health. However, what they also don't realize is that the relationship may not *always* be bad. This is part of the toxic nature. The abuse can be cyclical and follow a similar pattern. We will discuss this pattern further in the following sections, but the overarching idea is that the abuser may

be kind and loving one day, then abusive and harmful the next. The victim may never know which version of their partner to expect, leaving them hanging on hoping for another good day. This cyclical nature creates an addiction, as the victim becomes used to the highs and lows. They know, either consciously or subconsciously, that each time there is a low, it will be followed by another high. All of this will be discussed in the coming sections.

3. **Dependence.** This connects to betrayal trauma theory. Even when abuse is present, there may still be essential needs that the abusive partner is meeting, even in the negative portions of the cycles of abuse. Depending on how the victim grew up in childhood, they may simply not know how to form healthy attachments. If you were always in toxic and codependent relationships, then you might have fallen into one easily as an adult. This is not your fault, but it *is* something that has to be understood and something for you to be aware of in order to change.

4. **Threat Response.** When our body first encounters abuse, it can be a shocking experience. The way our body responds to any threat, even a perceived one, is the fight, flight, or freeze response. The stress hormones, adrenaline and cortisol, run through the body and trigger a reaction. However, in abusive situations, you may not feel like you can fight or flight safely. Therefore, you may freeze and stay in place. If you ignore your primal stress hormones and remain in the toxic situation, your body will learn that this is how you should react to such situations, thus increasing the probability of it happening later and strengthening the trauma bond. You might consciously be aware of the abuse, but you react as if it's not happening because it is easier to ignore it than it is to acknowledge the true danger of the situation you are in.

5. **Hormones.** Speaking of stress hormones, other types of hormones play a huge role in the effectiveness of a trauma bond. Dopamine is a hormone connected with positive feelings and it is released when we are feeling pleasure, something that is felt often in a romantic relationship through emotions and intimacy. This positive hormone helps us feel more attached to our partner, and it cultivates

feelings of trust and love. Another positive hormone is oxytocin, which is often released through physical affection and intimacy. This also helps to bond people. Oxytocin is released even during simple human interactions such as hugs. However, both of these hormones may work to your detriment in an abusive situation. After an incident of abuse, your partner may shower you with gifts or apologies. This releases dopamine and oxytocin, which prompt positive feelings, further strengthening your connection and trauma bond to your abuser. The negative hormones, adrenaline and cortisol, are typically released during incidents of abuse or when you walk on eggshells, trying not to upset your abuser. High levels of cortisol have been linked to a variety of mental and physical problems. This back and forth rush of hormones is confusing to the body and can lead to addiction.

All of these are plausible and valid reasons for a trauma bond to form, even when there is clear abuse going on. It's evident that there is an actual biochemical element to the relationship. The victim does not stay because they are too "weak" to leave. Those who have never been in an abusive situation simply do not understand the full effect of the feelings, highs, and lows. Now that we understand when a trauma bond can form and why, we will discuss the ways in which you can recognize if you are currently experiencing a trauma bond within your relationship.

Summary

- The scenarios in which trauma bonds most commonly form are in situations including domestic abuse, incest, kidnapping, human trafficking, and in cults, though they are also prevalent in romantic relationships that the victim feels obligated to maintain.
- For a trauma bond to form, four specific conditions must be met: the victim must perceive a threat from the abuser, any abuse must be followed by displays of kindness, the victim must be isolated from others, and the victim must believe that they are unable to leave the relationship, whether or not they are truly capable.

- Five reasons that trauma bonds may form in relationships include deep attachments between the victim and abuser; the cyclical nature of the abuse; the dependence of the victim on the abuser; freezing during a fight, flight, or freeze response; and the presence of positive hormones such as dopamine or oxytocin between cycles of abuse, which further bond victims to their abusers.

In the next section, you will learn the red flags and signs of trauma bonds in relationships, which will help you identify if you are currently in a trauma-bonded relationship.

Section 4: Understanding Gaslighting

The term Gaslighting originated from Patrick Hamilton's 1938 stage play entitled *Gas Light*. The story is about a husband trying to convince his wife that she is going insane by manipulating sounds and objects in the house and when she tries to validate them, he tells her she is being delusional. The word gaslighting refers to how the husband tries to dim the gas light in the house while pretending that it is not happening to make his wife doubt herself and her perception of the truth.

What is Gaslighting?

Gaslighting is a manipulative technique or a psychological form of abuse where an individual or group makes another person question his or her memories, sanity, and perception of the truth. Person experiencing anxiety, confusion, and self-doubt are easy preys of gaslighting.

Warning and signs of Gaslighting

Gaslighters are usually narcissists. They always demand attention and everything should always be about them. If they cannot sway you, they will start to torment you. If you try to leave them, they will manipulate you to pull you back. Beware if you see some the following signs:

- They project their flaws on you.
- They tell you people think you are crazy or tell you that you are crazy.
- They isolate you by saying your friends and family are bad influences.
- They often lie even without reason. When confronted with their lies, they deny it or counter that you are being paranoid or imagining things.

The intent of the gaslighter is to make you dependent on them for your version of reality.

Example of Gaslighting in action

Gaslighters plant seeds of doubts in the victim's mind to disorient and confuse them so they can gain control over them. Although gaslighting happens more commonly in romantic relationships, it can also happen within a family and in your own workplace. To understand more, here are illustrations of gaslighting in action.

Gaslighting in relationships

Gaslighting is very common between couples who are in a romantic relationship. The manipulator would make promises that he has no plans of keeping. When you follow up on it, he would deny saying it or would probably say you understood wrong. Another example is he would tell you information that he would later on deny making you think if he really said it or not. Example, you would say, *"I cooked shrimp pasta for you."* He would reply, *"You know I am allergic to shrimp."* Now you would think, when did he ever told you that? Sometimes he would follow it up with triangulation technique, *"My ex always remembers which food I'm allergic to."* So now on top of the doubt, you would feel guilty because it would seem that you are not giving importance to his needs.

Gaslighting within family

Your family is your best support system but unbelievably, gaslighting happens amongst family members. Children will naturally test boundaries set by their parents. Example, A child received a B minus in his report card, the parent will say, *"This is your fault, if you had been studying this wouldn't have happened. I told you to study. You know I cannot watch over you because I am busy with work. You never listen to me."*

The parent is passing on the blame of his or her shortcomings to the child. It will not help them if a parent blame them for "mucking up" or "misbehaving" instead of talking to them and teaching them the consequences of their action. Reinforcing their belief that they are not good enough will only instill fear to explore and later on stunt their growth and development.

Gaslighting at workplace

Gaslighting often succeeds when you lack self-confidence. It is designed to confuse you so they can maintain power over you. You can also find gaslighting at your workplace. It can come from a colleague or your own boss. Almost every boss wants to maximize their staff and to do that they can use gaslighting to make you comply. Example, Your boss tells you that working overtime can lead to a promotion, so you do it but only to find that another person was promoted. You confront your boss about it and his reply, *"I did not say if you work overtime you will surely get promoted. I said working overtime could* lead to a promotion. *Your other colleague worked overtime too; and was submitting her work before the deadline.*"

Another example, A jealous colleague can give you a hard time by trying to undermine you self-confidence. *"Oh didn't you receive the company memo? I'm sorry, I guess only few select people received a copy."*

Gaslighiting Techniques

Here are five most common gaslighting techniques employed by manipulators:

1. **Denial.** This is the number one technique used in gaslighting. The manipulator will deny saying anything or pretend that events did not happen. Example. "You are being paranoid, you know that's not true." or "Don't make up things."

2. **Countering.** The manipulator tries to question the victim's memories to confuse them. When the victim says something, the manipulator counter it with statements that would make the victim doubt his or her memory. Example, "Are you sure that is what happened?" or "You know you have a bad memory."

3. **Trivializing.** The manipulator scoffs off the victim's words; he or she belittles and disregard the victim's feelings. Example, "That's not what she said, you are just being too sensitive." or "You know you are over reacting right?"

4. **Stereotyping.** The manipulator intentionally uses negative stereotypes of the victim's race, ethnicity, sexuality, gender, or age to manipulate them. Example, "They will think you have AIDS because of you are gay." or "You have a session with a shrink? Do you have a mental problem?"

5. **Diverting.** The manipulator changes the subject of the discussion and instead questions the credibility of the victim. Example, "You can come up with a better idea than that." or "Did you get this harebrained idea from your crazy friends?"

Section 5: Basics of Dark Psychology in Seduction

In a relationship, both sexes find joy in pursuing their target, more so with men. The more difficult the challenge of the pursuit, the more worthwhile the rewards. Some prefer to be seduced and manipulated. However, not all seduction pursuits are positive. If the person has the "triad" personality traits, seduction can turn into a traumatic bond. Dark psychology in seduction creates bonds with the intention of inflicting psychological wounds.

Here are six examples of dark psychology in seduction techniques.

Regression seduction

Sigmund Freud defined regression as a defense mechanism that leads to long-term or temporary reversion of one's self-image to an earlier phase of development rather than face handling unwanted impulses. In psychology, regression occurs when an individual's behavior and personality reverts to the early stages of development and behaves in a childish manner.

Regression seduction is similar to DDLG or "Daddy Dom / Little Girl" roleplay in BDSM. In DDLG, one plays the role of the Daddy (Mom if female) and the other plays Little Girl (or Boy if male). The Dom is the superior in the relationship while the Little Girl is the submissive. The "little" undergoes age regression and the age depends on the time the "little" felt happy and content. Most of DDLG relationships are consensual role-play to spice up the relationship.

The strategy requires you to remind them of their childhood by playing the role of their parents and making them live through their oedipal dream. Example, scolding them like a parent would. Combine the scolding with an erotic component designed to seduce them into giving in to you.

Judge Seduction

In judge seduction, the seducer sets himself or herself up as superior, making the seduced chase for approval. The seducer can use subtle triangulation technique to create anxiety and discontent. If the seduced knows there is ongoing competition, they will try to seek ways to prove themselves to the seducer. Example, your man asked you to accompany him in their company party. He tells you *"This is a formal event and the females will be wearing long gowns. I'm sure you can find something appropriate to make me proud."* If he has control over you, your normal reaction is to be defensive and try to prove to him that you are worthy to stand beside him.

Traumatic Bonding

Trauma bonding is comparable to Stockholm syndrome where a person is loyal to a destructive person. In trauma bonding, the superior partner uses emotional and/or physical abuse to control and keep the other partner loyal to him or her. Trauma bonding is not limited to domestic abuse, it can also happen in hostage taking, kidnapping, cult organizations, incest or child abuse and at work. Example, a stepfather having sexual relations with his stepdaughter will tell her that it is something normal, she owes him because he provides all their needs, he will buy everything she wants or use threat to force her. Another example would be a husband verbally and physically abusing his wife to punish her for her "supposed" errors or undermining her self-confidence to the point that she is dependent on him. Attachment forms through the cycle of affectionate and destructive behavior by the abuser.

Emotional Roller-Coaster Bonding

Emotional roller-coaster bonding is somewhat similar to traumatic bonding except that manipulator uses emotional abuse to control. The manipulator uses a "love you-hate you" kind of abuse. One moment the manipulator is very loving and sweet and the next he is demeaning and insulting. The manipulator employs yelling, triangulations, isolation, undermining self-confidence, or a combination of other emotional tactics. Once down, the manipulator pacifies the target by showering her with affection and love. This makes the target feel grateful to the manipulator. The cycle continues until the target becomes attached to the manipulator, and stays waiting and hoping for the payoff, the showering of love and affection.

Control Through Personal Kinks

The manipulator provides the target sexual satisfaction through kinks. The target usually keeps their sexual kinks a secret and only the manipulator is aware of it. This gives

the manipulator an advantage and making him or her the only person who can sexually satisfy them. This seduction technique is common in BDSM. After the movie *"Fifty Shades of Gray"* BDSM acceptance has increased although many who are into BDSM would disagree that the movie captured the real essence of the lifestyle. Despite the increase in acceptance, many still hide that they arc into this lifestyle. Example, a Teacher who gets sexual satisfaction through spanking would not want that secret revealed. He or she would be dependent on her lover to provide the sexual kink because giving the lover full control over her.

Love Bombing

In a relationship, it is common for a partner (often the man) to try impressing the other partner. Dinner dates, flowers, gifts, sweet words, and other surprises are normal stuff that a man use to woo, seduce, and impress. However, when a man starts bombarding you with *excessive* affection, gifts, attention, flattery, praises it turns into a seductive tactic called love bombing. The key word here is *"excessive,"* When the person is going over the top with his affections, splurges on out of town dates, expensive jewelries and vacations, even if you just met, you should become alert. There are two types of love bombers; one is the desperate and needy love bomber who forms an unhealthy attachment to their target but tend to have genuine feelings. The other type is the sinister love bomber or the narcissist sociopath who deliberately employs strategies designed to control their target.

Section 6: Basics of Dark Psychology In Relationship

After dating and all the conflicts it entails, you are now in the relationship stage. There is less conflict in relationship than in dating but now comes the biggest problem; keeping your partner hooked into you.

Psychological Tools of Female Control

Women use typically three types of games to get their man. First is getting them hook game, second is getting a commitment game and lastly the relationship power game. The last being the hardest to accomplish. How do you keep them hooked into you?

So how do women control men in a relationship? The top three frames that women set up to control the relationship.

1. Set up a "you are expected to provide for me" frame whereby men are expected to provide and cater to the women's needs
2. Set up "judge frames" where men's worthiness and value are assessed base on their ability to provide and cater to the women's needs.
3. Set up relationship prize frame where women position themselves as the more valuable part of the relationship.

Women tend to set up the frames of reference in the relationship; what is proper and not, what is good and wrong, and what standards of behavior to be followed. Men rarely challenge these frames and end up playing by the women's rules.

To enforce the rules, women uses compliance tools on men to become the relationship lead allowing her to *task* him. What are these tools?

Nagging and Drama

Nagging works with rewards and punishments. If you are good, you are rewarded if not then you suffer the nagging wrath. Nagging is a long term behavioral changing tool and sets the priority of what is important while drama sets the priority of what is urgent.

Drama becomes powerful with the use of emotions. Women use passion and emotions with the right amount of self-righteousness that tells men "I am right," Nagging combined with drama are tools of punishment and compliance of the judge power frame.

Blaming and Criticism

Women love using these verbal aggression tool because it puts the men on a defensive and when they do, it communicates to the women that they are guilty, confirms that he exist to serve and make her happy, and that she is totally in charge.

Men are just caught dumbfounded by the outburst and the lashing and often reacts predictably. Their response from getting defensive, trying to fix the problem, make excuses, fight with them, ask the women to calm down and tries to understand the real problem.

Shaming

Shaming is probably the most powerful aggression and compliance tool used by women. Shame leverages the need for basic respect and worthy of love. Shame punishments includes isolation, scorn, and igniting the feelings of unworthiness. When women shames men, it attacks their manhood. It cuts them deeply, questioning their masculinity. Some of the most powerful shaming words that cripples men are *impotent, weak, "pussy", and unsuccessful.*

Tasking

Drama, shaming, nagging, and criticism are merely tools to get to the core of how women really control men; tasking. The more the men executes the tasks the more they are likely to invest and commit in a relationship. Tasking usually starts early on in the relationship. It can be as innocent as asking you to get her a cup of coffee or maybe ask you to carry her things. Other women hold off on the tasking until their power increases. As the relationship progresses, the demands dramatically increases.

It is the nature of men to chase and women assess. The hunter-prey dynamics between men and women warps the mindset of men. They feel as if they hit the jackpot once the chase is over. Thus, when men finally get into the relationship, their mindset attuned to accepting the women's demands.

Males techniques for mate-control

Abusive men think that they have the right to control their partners. They have the right over how they think, what they should think, what they should say, and how they should act and behave. Their words is law and believe they are the only one entitled to allow and remove their partners' freedom.

This all boils down to what mindset of "Alpha-Beta" roles society imposed. The Alpha male is confident, dominant, daring, doesn't give a damn about anything. As a result, they command respect, leads, and they are independent and the Alpha male holds his frame.

The Beta male is unassuming, shy, defers to others, cares deeply about others' opinion of him, socially awkward, shy, weak, small, and unlike the alpha does not hold his frame. Most males are beta males because it is a biological tendency.

Control is exercised using both psychological and physical tools like criticism, saying that their controlling behavior is for your best interest, pretending hurt by your behavior and non-stop complaining.

Possessiveness

They employ different tactics to keep you to himself like isolation and guilt tripping. Keeping their partner isolated makes it easier for manipulators to control their partners. They usually excuse this behavior as "doing it for your good,"

Entitlement

Manipulators feel they are entitled to everything in the relationship. They give them freedom and only they are entitled to take it back. Manipulators feel they are entitled to have their partner even if they do not want them. They are entitled to have their partner serve and take care of them.

Subtle Manipulations

Control is not limited to verbal or physical intimidation. Manipulators employ mental games and power moves to control their partner. Some of these manipulative tactics include:

- Blaming his sins on you.
- Divide and conquer tactic, albeit turning you against family and friends.
- Gaslighting to drive you insane and make you doubt yourself
- Keeping you out of sort with his mood swings.

Section 1: How to Recognize a Trauma Bond

There are countless signs of a trauma bond. They can be something big that is hard to ignore, or they can be something small that you find in the everyday routines in your life with your partner. Sometimes, you might even just get a gut feeling that won't go away, and you may simply *feel* that something is wrong. No matter how perfect things may seem on a given day, something feels *off*. This can also be a sign. Let's look at some signs that you may be forming a trauma bond in your relationship.

1. **You're constantly worried about upsetting them.** When you have formed a trauma bond with your abuser, you might feel like you have to constantly "walk on eggshells" when you're around them. You may constantly feel that something could go wrong at any minute, even if you don't know exactly why. You may even be *aware* that they are the one at fault for any harm or damage done to your relationship, yet you still feel the need to be careful. While being cautious around them, you may hide your true feelings from them. When something upsets you, you keep it inside, because the satisfaction and emotional validation that may come from the interaction in a healthy relationship is not likely to be obtained in your situation. In fact, you know that telling them might "set them off", which is the opposite of the desired effect.

2. **You feel the need to prove yourself.** This pairs well with the first sign in that, even though you may *know* that your partner is the toxic one, you still feel like you have to prove your loyalty to them. This may still ring true even if you are doing everything you can to keep the relationship functioning. You may be enduring abuse and accepting all kinds of betrayal, but you still find yourself being questioned and accused by your abuser.

3. **You feel responsible for their behavior.** People who are trauma-bonded to their abusers often take on the blame for what their partners do inside and outside of their relationship. As these victims have been strongly conditioned to put their abuser's needs first, they will often do anything to ensure that their partners are okay. Occasionally, the abused may publicly make excuses for their abuser or take on the blame if the abuse happens in public and others question it.

If the victim's friends or family display concern about the situation, the victim may instinctively jump to diffuse and minimize their concerns by taking responsibility and shifting blame for their abuser's actions either to themselves or to an external source to make their abuser seem like less of a threat. These are some common excuses made by victims to minimize concerns about their abuse:

- "Well, they just had a bad childhood."
- "No, I deserved it because…"
- "Not everyone could put up with me either!"
- "They have been getting so much better since we've been together."
- "Oh, their jealousy just gets the best of them sometimes."

4. **You feel addicted to your abuser.** Many trauma-bonded victims have noted that they actually felt an addiction to their abuser. When they were away from them for too long, they experienced an unexplainable pull back to them. While many ask abuse victims "How could you go back?", their choice to return to an abusive situation can be explained by this. The hormones involved in a trauma bond have a great deal to do with this feeling of addiction. Being in an abusive relationship can cause "ups and downs"; while things can be really bad for a while, they can cycle around to be really good, too. This is all part of the toxic abuse cycle, which we will discuss in the coming sections. However, when the brain of the victim gets used to this rollercoaster, an addiction to their abuser will form. With stress, there is a rush of cortisol. Then, when the cycle flips and things are good again, dopamine replaces the cortisol, causing pleasure and happy feelings. The brain becomes accustomed to feeling a negative hormone and tries to downplay its severity, all with the subconscious knowledge that dopamine will soon come flooding back. This causes you to believe you are deeply in love with a person who is abusing and hurting you and can cause victims to crave that high so strongly that they are willing to suffer the lows.

5. **You have low self-esteem.** Throughout the abusive relationship and formation of a trauma bond, you may actually forget who you once were. It will feel like you are a different version of yourself. After compromising so much of

what you love and are passionate about, it will be hard to maintain high self-esteem. You may have even been very confident before this relationship and are now finding that your confidence is gone. Almost everything in your life is filtered through this relationship. Many toxic and abusive individuals seek out confident and strong people because these are traits they lack within themselves. Nowadays, however, you may notice that you are the one constantly building them up while they tear you down. But, you still can't let go. Not only this, but the constant fight to prove yourself to the abuser is exhausting and you are starting to lose faith in yourself.

6. **You desire emotional support and affection from your abuser.** As stated before, the relationship may have started amazingly. But now, you have to fight for their time and affection. They give you little crumbs and pieces of their love to keep you hooked. Many trauma bonds are intense; while the sex may be strong and high intensity, the actual affection, such as hand-holding and gentle physical touch, is sparse. It may feel like you can't emotionally connect with your abuser any more, even though you are desperately trying to. You might feel invisible, like you are all alone in the relationship. This only adds to your feelings of low self-esteem as you wonder, *what's wrong with me?*

7. **You feel crazy!** A trauma-bonded relationship is designed to make you lose trust in yourself and feel crazy. In a relationship filled with accusations, spying, and paranoia, there is no room for security or comfort. As the abuse continues and escalates, you might feel a cognitive dissonance happening. You might start having panic attacks, nightmares, or even a fear of going out anywhere in public. You begin doubting your own sanity and only believe what the abuser says, even though you know, deep inside, that they cannot be trusted.

8. **It wasn't always bad.** We've all heard the analogy of the frog in hot water. If relationships are abusive from the beginning, the victim has a high likelihood of recognizing the abuse and escaping the situation. However, many victims, especially those suffering from trauma bonds, recall that their relationship "wasn't always bad!" Many times, it was actually *great* in the beginning, and the

victim will recall an abundance of affection, gifts, and happy memories. However, the water was slowly heated to the point that they have now reached a boiling point where they *have* to get out.

Phew! These signs are difficult to absorb. A trauma-bonded relationship is an extremely toxic and psychologically damaging situation. If you recognize these signs in your relationship, hopefully, you can find some solace knowing that you are not alone in these feelings and symptoms. Victims of abuse have similar psychological responses to the unhealthy situation they are in.

If these signs feel all too familiar but you're still not sure if you're in a trauma-bonded relationship, we will use test questions to see if you have really entered a trauma bond.

Summary

- There are many signs of a trauma-bonded relationship, but many victims experience similar psychological responses.
- Victims of trauma-bonded abusive relationships tend to experience loss of self-esteem, feelings of being "crazy", and a need to make excuses for their abuser.

In the next section, you can take a test to see how trauma-bonded you are in your relationship.

Section 2: Trauma Bond Test

Now that we have gone over the most common signs of the trauma bond, we can take a test to see how many of the symptoms you may be experiencing right now. The test consists of several "yes" or "no" questions that are specific to *your* feelings within the relationship. Try to answer them honestly and really think about the true nature of your relationship. We often try to sugarcoat abuse in our relationships, but this is a safe space for you to begin being honest with yourself and learn how to identify the hurtful actions you have been suffering from your abuser.

1. Do you make excuses for your partner's abusive behavior?
2. Do you feel like you always "owe" the abuser something, even though they are the one causing harm to you?
3. Does it feel like you and your partner have a serious need for each other?
4. Is it hard to go more than a day or two without seeing your abuser?
5. Is your relationship chaotic? Does each day bring out a different side of your partner?
6. Is the sex intense?
7. Do you find yourself sacrificing your own time and needs in order to be with the abuser or to satisfy them in some way?
8. Do you have to "cover-up" physical or emotional abuse when you are around people who care about your health and safety?
9. Do you secretly believe that you can help the abuser get better and feel happy? Do you think that you can fix them in some way?
10. Is there constant suspicion and paranoia in the relationship from both you and the abuser?
11. Does it feel like something is "off", but you're not sure what it is?
12. Are you finding it hard to be your true self in the relationship?
13. Are you hiding parts of yourself in order to avoid upsetting your abuser?
14. Are you afraid to leave the relationship?
15. Are you constantly fighting for affection from the abuser?

16. Does it feel like you are "losing your mind" and starting to doubt your own decision-making abilities?

If you answered yes to most of these questions, then you are likely trauma-bonded to your partner. As you may have noted, many of these questions pertain to the "intensity" of the relationship. This is an important aspect of a trauma bond, as, without the intensity, the relationship would likely lack the highs and lows and the persistent feeling that it might get better.

Summary

- It can be difficult to know if you are really in a trauma bond, especially if you are currently experiencing the symptoms.
- Many symptoms of a trauma bond pertain to the intensity of feelings in the relationship.
- If you answered yes to several of the above questions, then you are likely in a trauma bond.

If this test has revealed to you that you are in a trauma bond, you may be wondering how this happened to you. In the next section, you will learn the stages that lead up to the formation of a trauma bond.

Section 3: The Seven Stages of Trauma Bond Formation

In any toxic or abusive relationship, there are various stages that repeat in a cyclical pattern that must be at play in order for the relationship to continue. These stages force the victim through intense highs followed by crushing lows, always with the hope that it will be followed by another high. It is this push and pull that will keep the victim hooked, or trauma-bonded, to both the relationship and to the abusive individual. This creates a constant state of confusion and uncertainty for the victim, which is crucial to the abuser's maintenance of control in the relationship; they know that the victim will stay, all with the hope that one day, things will get better. Many individuals stuck in these relationships are not aware that this cycle is happening to them. This is especially true for children whose parents are abusive, as they are likely far too young to recognize abuse. However, if you are in a stage of life where you are able to recognize these things, we will now help you put a name to the stages that have hooked you into your current situation. To understand how to exit such a situation, you must understand how you landed there in the first place.

Stage #1: Love, love, love!

Many abuse victims nostalgically recall the beautiful beginnings of their relationship and sadly wonder "why can't things just go back to the way they were?" While many will believe that this is the victim looking back with rose-colored glasses, oftentimes things really *were* amazing at the beginning of such a relationship. This connection is usually very intense; often referred to as "love bombing," the abuser and victim form a bond that may make the victim feel like they have finally found "the one". Either party may tell the other that they "have never experienced something like this before", or that they see their partner as "one-of-a-kind". This stage is all about building up the victim and placing them on such a high pedestal that they are not prepared to fall. While overwhelming the victim with affection, future abusers may say things such as:

- "I've finally met my soulmate!"
- "You are the most gorgeous person I've ever seen."
- "I didn't believe in love until I met you."
- "I don't deserve someone as amazing as you."

Note that *all of the above statements* emphasize the unique and one-of-a-kind nature of either the victim or of their connection and relationship to the abuser.

Stage #2: Trust & Dependency

During the second stage of trauma bond formation, the abuser will do everything to gain the victim's trust, as well as everything they can to learn more about the victim. This is the "research" phase, in which they will start asking questions and wanting to know everything about their victim. Rather than doing this to know and appreciate their partner better, they do this to equip themselves to exploit their victim's deepest insecurities and know how to push their buttons. However, while they are still in a positive stage of this cyclical relationship, they will refrain from showing their hand. In the meantime, they will go out of their way to show how loyal they are and how much the victim can depend on them, attempting to form a codependent bond. **Codependency** forms when two people are too reliant and invested in the other and become unable to function independently anymore. This is the basis of a trauma bond: both the abuser *and* the abused need one another. The abused becomes reliant and dependent on the abuser for love and affection, and the abuser relies on their ability to put down the abused in order to feel confident in themselves.

Stage #3: The Big Pivot from Love to Criticism

In this stage, the abuser begins to show their true colors, and everything that was said and built up in the first stage slowly melts away. The criticism usually begins slowly and is so minute at first that it can easily be written off. However, with time, many things that the abuser once praised in their partner will now become targets for criticism and ridicule. The abuser will slowly shift all blame for all issues in the relationship onto the shoulders of the victim, and they will start blaming their own feelings and perceptions of the world—clearly, things that are removed from the victim—on the actions of the abused. This is unfair, and not the fault of the victim, but because they have a relationship with this person that was once so loving and intense, they will do all that they can to get back to that stage. This will put a strain on the victim because their abuser's demands will only escalate as they ask their victim to compromise their entire being.

Stage #4: Gaslighting & Projection

We spoke a bit about gaslighting in the earlier. As a reminder, **gaslighting** is a way in which the abuser alters the narrative of their actions in an attempt to alter the victim's reality into something that will shift blame away from the abuser. Let's look at a hypothetical example; your partner has suddenly become very critical and abusive toward you. You confront them, asking why this change has occurred. Your partner then denies that they have criticized or abused you, calling you crazy or implying that you have memory problems in an attempt to make you doubt your reality. Because this can lead to victims doubting their own perception of reality and relying on their abuser for an "accurate" account of events, it can be extremely difficult to know if this is happening to you while you are being actively gaslighted. Some common phrases that gaslighters may use include the following:

- "You're way too sensitive."
- "You're only saying that because you're insecure."
- "You are *seriously* crazy—get some help."
- "Don't be so dramatic."
- "That literally never happened."
- "I never said that."
- "It's all in your head."

While it can be very difficult for a victim to realize this, it is *critical* that they know that they aren't crazy and their abuse is not only happening in their head. These mind games can be extremely psychologically and emotionally damaging to the victim.

Take another look at the list of common phrases above. You may notice that all of the phrases work to place blame and doubt on the victim, remove blame or doubt from the abuser, or both. This is because a critical component of gaslighting is to shift the blame from the abuser onto their victim through a technique called projection. **Projection** is when someone places their own thoughts, feelings, or actions onto another person, and by doing so, the abuser makes everything their victim's problem instead of their own.

Stage #5: Giving in

At this stage, many victims simply feel exhausted. They have tried to insert reality into the world of the abuser, but it isn't working. However, they fondly recall the good beginnings and do not want to leave, hoping to fix their relationship and bring it back to its former glory. This is the influence of the trauma bond. Many victims in this stage feel that they can still "save" their partner and their relationship, and furthermore, they might still love their abuser as well. And there's nothing wrong with that—these victims are human, with real and honest emotions. However, the abuser is aware of this and will exploit it. In this stage, victims may have decided to give in to their abuser's ideals and try their best to appease them. They may find themselves isolated and cut off from family members and friends in order to keep their abuser happy. They might give up time that would normally be dedicated to exercising or pursuing their passions in order to ensure that everything is okay within their relationship.

Step #6: Losing Yourself

Now that the victim has fallen deep into their abuser's world and mind games, they will struggle to know who they are more than ever. It can feel like they are a shadow of who they once were. They may be painfully aware at this stage that something is terribly wrong, but they either don't want to or know how to fix it. In fact, they may have lost their confidence so much that they are unable to fight back at all. The abuse may have escalated so much that they no longer recognize their partner at all. At this stage, many victims are simply doing their best to avoid fighting.

Stage #7: Addiction

The final stage, which doubles as a huge red flag for a trauma-bonded relationship, is that the victim feels an addiction to the abuser and the feelings associated with the relationship. Their body is functioning at a constant level of stress and desperation. But still, they are thrown bread crumbs of affection and love; because of the sharp contrast to the abuse and negativity, these crumbs will feel like nothing that the victim has ever experienced before. Because of this, they may think that this is better than any other relationship they've ever had and choose to stay.

These stages can repeat multiple times. The first time a victim experiences them can be shocking and confusing, but immediately following this shock and upset, their partner may suddenly revert back to the "good" person they once were and begin love-bombing their victim again. Sadly, this plays into the effect of the gaslighting, convincing the victim that the previous abuse may have all been in their head, after all. However, these cyclical stages are what all trauma-bonded victims experience.

Summary

- There are several cyclical stages that lead to the formation of a trauma bond between a victim and an abuser.
- The stages begin with positivity and end with negativity and center heavily on the influences of gaslighting and projection.

In the next section, you will learn the key differences between trauma bonding and real love.

Section 4: Trauma Bonding versus Real Love

The emotions associated with a trauma bond are often confused with real love due to their comparable intensities. However, real love is *not* abusive, and it is *not* toxic. The victim and their partner may share intimate life details and similar interests, but none of this constitutes love on its own. A trauma bond creates a relationship full of confusion, hurt, and insecurity, whereas love creates a relationship full of understanding, kindness, and acceptance. This is important to understand so that victims may begin to recognize the differences between a healthy relationship and a toxic connection while they are in the midst of a trauma bond.

1. **Love is patient.** Love does not put pressure on anything. Love is patient and waits, in every sense of the word. Someone who truly loves you does not put pressure on you to do anything you are uncomfortable with yet. They would wait for you to be ready for anything and accept you as you are. If you are unsure if you are bonded to someone by love or by a trauma bond, you should ask yourself if your partner is patient with you. Your partner should want the best for you and understand that we all do things on our own time.

2. **Love is accepting.** In a trauma bond, you may find that you compromise integral aspects of yourself and your life to please your partner. This is not how real love should be; while real love may require that individuals work to improve themselves and to be better partners, it should never make you fundamentally change who you are. You know yourself well enough to realize when you are altering your true self and morals in order to appease someone else. This often happens in a trauma bond. If you are unsure if you are in a trauma bond, you should ask yourself if you have felt compelled by your partner to change your way of dressing, your behavior, or even who you spend your time with in order to appease them. If you find your partner compelling you to do any of these things, this is a sign that you are trauma-bonded and not in a loving relationship.

3. **Love is understanding.** If you have a bad day or if you can't meet an expectation, love understands this. On the other hand, if you are in a trauma bond, your partner may attack your very character and put you down when you

make a mistake. This is unfair to you, and their reactions should not be something that *you* have to fix. Instead, this is a direct reflection of the abuser's unrealistic and unhealthy expectations for their victim. Many toxic individuals can only see an individual in either a positive or a negative light at any given time, removing room for nuance or understanding when people make mistakes. This is something we will talk about in more depth in the coming sections, but if you find that your partner or parent hates you one day and loves you the next, you can be certain that it is not really genuine love.

4. **Love has empathy.** Empathy includes understanding others, but it is so much more than that. Being empathetic toward others means that you place yourself in another person's shoes and think about how your actions will make them feel. It's about being aware of how your actions and words may come off to another person. While a lack of empathy does not inherently mean anything bad about an individual—some types of neurodivergency make people struggle with empathy without making them bad people—abusers either lack empathy or they see how their actions impact you and do not care; they're only concerned with their own wants and needs. Their needs will always be a priority to them, regardless of whether you're having a bad day or feeling sad. They *will* find a way to make the situation about them. If you find that every time you express yourself to your partner or parent they try to twist the situation back on themselves, this is not love. Someone who loves you would listen to you and focus on how *you* are feeling when you need the attention. They would want you to feel better and would do all they can to help.

5. **Love makes you feel secure.** If you are with an abuser, you may feel insecure most of the time; love should *not* make you feel this way. Love is about constant security. However, a trauma bond is about keeping you on the edge, where adrenaline and cortisol are running high. You might always have a negative "gut feeling" that is nagging away at you when you are with your abuser or talking to them. However, when you are around someone who genuinely loves you, they

should make you feel safe and secure. They should be a safe haven away from the other stressors of the world rather than being the reason for your insecurity.

If you are still feeling unsure about whether or not your relationship is bonded by love or trauma, ask yourself the following questions:

- Does your partner put your needs before theirs when you really need them to?
- Do you and your partner trust one another when you aren't together?
- Are you realistic about expectations for each other within your relationship?
- Do you feel like you are part of a team?
- Can you and your partner enjoy your time together?
- Do you feel safe around them?
- Does it feel like you are constantly growing in your relationship?

Just like with the trauma bond test, if you answer yes to most of these questions, then you are most likely in a loving relationship. While no relationship is perfect, there is a clear line between healthy and unhealthy. All of us have our flaws! But, when we choose a partner, we decide to accept them. And, if the toxic person in our life happened to be a caregiver, they were *supposed* to care for us and love us unconditionally. Children will make mistakes and have a growing period. If you can't say "yes" to many of the questions, take a moment to really think about the questions and imagine what it would be like to say yes and feel loved unconditionally. Think about what you want going forward. Real love cannot be outdone by any kind of trauma bond. It may be hard to imagine what it feels like right now, but living a life free of toxic connections is the only healthy way to live.

Summary

- Relationships bonded by trauma and relationships bonded by love are drastically different.
- Trauma bonding creates a relationship filled with insecurities while healthy love creates a stable and secure relationship.
- If you are trying to distinguish whether your relationship is based on healthy love, refer to the list of questions to help clarify your thoughts.

In the next section, you will learn more about the cycle of abuse and how it takes hold in a trauma-bonded relationship.

Section 5: The Continuous Cycle of Abuse

We have now covered the seven stages that lead to the formation of a trauma bond. Once the trauma bond is formed, the victim will be trapped in an endless cycle of abuse as long as the relationship continues, and this will last until the victim is able to end it. The abuser will *rarely* be the one to end the relationship, as they enjoy the power that comes with having someone to inflict their abuse upon. This cycle pertains to all kinds of abusive relationships; parents use this on their children and partners use it on their significant others. The phases of an abusive cycle can be broken down into four stages: tension, abuse, reconciliation, and calm. We will discuss each in detail, using the hypothetical example of Anna and Tom to illustrate each stage.

Stage #1: Tension

In this part of the cycle, tensions are running high. There is likely something the abuser is focusing on in the victim's behavior that is causing them to become increasingly angry. However, this is not to be confused with blame lying on the victim; it is *not* the victim's fault that the tensions are rising. Many times, this tension is coming from an unrealistic expectation not being met, or from a perceived slight. This is all in the abuser's head, but they will attempt to make it the fault and problem of the victim through projection. Once tension starts rising, the abuser will begin latching onto it, and the victim may notice changes in their behavior, speech, or attitude.

Example: Anna and Tom have been together for a few months. In the beginning, he didn't care if she went out without him, but now he hates it and he tells her it's because he "doesn't trust other men". Because of this, she hasn't been out without him in a very long time. She only goes places with Tom, and he will usually accompany her even when she is going out with her friends. However, it's her best friend's birthday and she is planning to go out with all her girlfriends. They want to make it a "girls' night", and none of their boyfriends are coming. This is perceived as an insult to Tom and he begins acting distant and seeming anxious. Anna has an idea about why he is distant, but she doesn't want to ask out of fear of how he will react.

In this scenario, we see Tom as an insecure individual that is trying to control what Anna does and when she goes out. Anna's decision to go out without him is giving him a great deal of anxiety because he knows he will be unable to control both her and the situation around her. Tom's reaction is in no way Anna's fault; she has every right to go out alone with her friends. However, Tom will perceive this as an insult and the tension will rise. This scenario will set off the first phase of the abuse cycle.

Stage #2: Abuse

This is when the abuse actually takes place. Whether it be physical, mental, or emotional, the abuser will begin to cause harm to the victim in the second phase. This is how the abuser releases the tension from the previous phase and attempts to feel better about themselves. They may rage, physically harm, or emotionally abuse the other person in an attempt to make them feel bad about what they "did", even though the victim is not to blame.

Example: While Anna is out with her friends, Tom starts calling her. She misses several of her phone calls because she is busy enjoying her time. However, she notices halfway through the night that he has been calling and listens to several of his messages. The messages are nasty; he calls her names and accuses her of cheating on him. When she comes home later that night, he begins yelling, screaming, and accusing her again of cheating. He calls her terrible names and tells her to leave the house, even though they live together. She begs him to let her stay and promises that she wasn't doing anything wrong. She does all she can to convince him that she had been loyal.

In this scenario, it's clear to see that Tom is both mentally and emotionally abusive toward Anna. Because she did not "listen" to his wishes for her to stay home, he called her and created a false situation to justify his anger. It was unfair for Tom to expect Anna to answer his calls, and it was unfair of him to project his feelings onto her and make her feel responsible for his jealousy. Tom was completely in the wrong here, ruining Anna's night and making the whole situation about him.

Stage #3: Reconciliation

In this part of the cycle, the abuser tries to apologize for their actions. They may even blame the other parts of the cycle, such as the tensions that built up, for their actions. They will talk about it obsessively as if it somehow makes up for the abuse they caused to their victim. It's important to remember that the abuser does *not* think logically about the abuse they inflict during the cycle; they truly believe that it was warranted. They think that their victim deserves it for how they acted. This is where the love-bombing begins again, and the abuser will use anything to lure their victim back. They might bring home jewelry, flowers, or their victim's favorite food, all while offering false promises of changing for the better. In this phase, many victims decide to forgive their abusers and resign to the false idea that it will never happen again.

Example: After ruining Anna's night, Anna decides it might be time to end the relationship. She tells him that she is done and leaves the house, staying with her friend for a week. During this time, Tom will not stop calling her and begging for her to come back. He tells her that he is sorry and it will never happen again. He promises to change. He blames the whole situation on the tension and says they just need to connect more. She will not respond, so he brings flowers to her work and continues to text and call her to apologize. He tries all he can to repair the relationship. At first, Anna stays strong, but eventually, she feels a pull back to him and decides to take him back. She feels it may have been a one-time thing, and she doesn't want to end their relationship over just one thing.

In this phase, we see the abuser lying to get the victim back, and we also see it working. Anna tries to avoid taking him back at first, but he sadly ropes her back in. The pull that she feels to return to him, even though he has verbally and emotionally abused her, is due to the trauma bond that connects the abuser and the victim.

Stage #4: Calm

In the last part of the cycle, there will be a period of calm. The victim will be able to rest easy, as there will be a bit of a break before the cycle starts up again. However, remember that the cycle will always continue as long as the victim is in a relationship with the abuser. There will always be another tension after the calm. The only way to end this cycle for good is to decide to put the relationship to rest. The abuser will continue to hurt the victim and attempt to reconcile for as long as they can.

Example: After reconnecting, things are better than ever with Tom and Anna. Tom suggests that they go away for the weekend in order to be alone together and get away from all the "stress" of their daily life. They go away and have a great time, and Anna tells all of her friends that he stuck to his promises to improve and that they are so in love.

Tom's suggestion that they go away after his abusive phase has two dangerous functions in the abuse cycle: first, this will further isolate Anna and entrap her, and second, this falls under love bombing. Instead of the adrenaline and cortisol which is active during abuse, there will be dopamine, oxytocin, and plenty of pleasurable feelings. This will strengthen the trauma bond between Anna and Tom, strengthening her psychological addiction to his cyclical abuse. Anna believes everything that Tom has said. However, another tension will arise eventually, and the cycle will, inevitably, repeat again.

Summary

- There are four main parts to the cycle of abuse: tension, abuse, reconciliation, and calm.
- The tension in the relationship will build up to a breaking point when the abuse happens, then the abuser will backtrack and try to reconcile.
- The only way to end the cycle is by ending the relationship.

In the next section, you will learn how the abuser uses idealization and devaluation in order to abuse and control the victim.

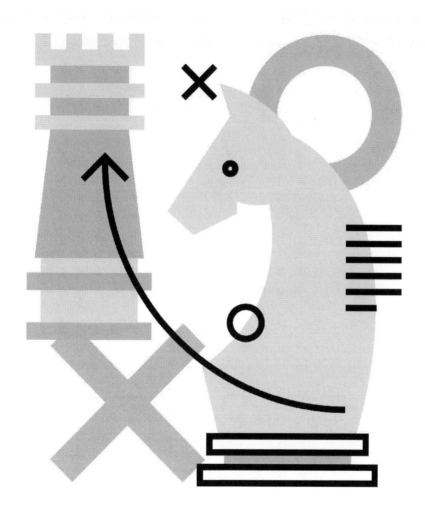

Section 1: Control Through Idealization & Devaluation

Do you ever feel like your abuser loves you one day but hates you the next? This is how the abuser keeps control over you. You may feel that their moods are simply affected by what is going on in their life, but it is truly something much deeper. In order to maintain control over both the victim and the relationship, the abuser knows that they must keep the victim in a state of confusion. There can be no consistency in the relationship. When the victim never knows what will come next, they will "behave" and do all they can to keep things in the "calm" phase. This includes avoiding any tensions that could set off the cycle of abuse.

The cycle of idealization and devaluation is a cycle within itself. **Idealization** is when your abuser may hold you on a pedestal, calling you amazing and complimenting everything you do. You will feel like you are on top of the world, and the abuser will be the one placing you there. Then, seemingly overnight, they switch, and they **devalue** you, putting down your character and those very same things they once loved about you. This back and forth is known as **splitting**. Splitting refers to a black and white way of thinking; it's either all good or all bad! This can refer to life events, other people, or work. Those who "split" often have personality disorders such as borderline personality disorder or narcissism. They are unable to see things as a combination of good and bad.

Those who split have no ability to recognize a mixed view of a person. This means that people in their lives are not allowed to be imperfect. They must always be behaving how they are expected to, or the abuser will become agitated. At any given time, they will only view their victim in a positive or negative light. It's important to look at how each stage works and why this maintains power over the victim. The phrases surrounding this cycle are also important to recognize, as many victims may be enduring this cycle without realizing it.

Idealization. This phase will sound similar to the love-bombing phase. It may appear that you can say and do no wrong. You and your partner are in love again, or you feel like your parents are finally proud of you and acknowledging your good qualities and hard work. This usually happens during the calm phase of the abuse cycle; there are no tensions or stressors causing the abuser to become upset. Some common phrases surrounding idealization:

- "You are so amazing! No one is better than you."

- "I love your personality."
- "Fate brought us together."
- "You're the only person in this whole world that I like."

Or, an abusive parent may say to their child:

- "You did great in school! You are so smart."
- "Your grades have been amazing lately!"
- "I'm so lucky I got a great kid like you."
- "You're so much smarter than the other kids your age."

Compliments are a natural and healthy part of human interaction, *but this is just the problem.* Abusers will use this healthy way of bonding and communicating in order to lure in their victims and create a false sense of security. Instead of saying anything genuine, they are saying what they believe that their victim wants to hear. They know that their victim is desperate for reassurance in the relationship and will grab onto this positive reinforcement.

Devaluation. In this stage, we see everything the abuser said in the idealization phase being torn down. They now see the victim in a harsh light. Sometimes, this switch can happen after a tension, similar to the one we talked about in the previous section, or it can happen due to a perceived slight. Trauma bonds are all about power. You may not be able to physically see the imbalance, but it is always there. This is why the devaluation state will hurt so much for the victim. They crave the approval and love of their abuser, whether the abuser is a parent or a partner. Oftentimes, the devaluing phrases are veiled, giving the abuser room to try to manipulate their victim into thinking they've simply "heard things wrong" or are overreacting. But their victim is *not* overreacting; it is seriously unhealthy to be amazing to someone one day and act as their enemy the next. Devaluation might sound like this:

- "You're way too sensitive; I didn't know you were like this!"
- "You tricked me into thinking you were an amazing person."
- "Your insecurities are really showing lately. It's not attractive."
- "Something is seriously wrong with you."
- "You're going to leave me, just like everyone else."

Between a parent and child, it might sound like:

- "What happened to your grades? I thought you were smart."
- "I don't even know why I had you."
- "The other kids are doing much better than you."
- "What's wrong with you?"

An abuser may even try to devalue the other relationships in your life during this phase:

- "You're so selfish, spending all of your time with your friends."
- "Your friends aren't good enough for you."
- "Your whole family is seriously crazy; why do you still see them?"
- "Your friends don't even like me, so why do you hang out with them?"

All of these things are extremely damaging and hurtful to the victim and create a sense of confusion. If this happens to you, you may be left wondering *what happened?* Take a moment and think about what a week in your life is like with this abuser. Go through each day of the week; were you in the devaluation or idealization phase on Monday? What about Tuesday? Maybe you cycle through multiple phases in one day, even. When the abuse is extreme, victims may experience this cycle many times during a day or week. This can be exhausting and tear away at their will to fight back to get away from the toxic environment.

Recognizing this cycle is a vital first step to learning to fight back so you can escape your abuse. If victims are unable to recognize this, they may continue to take on the blame for their abuser's behavior. They might think the tensions which set off their abuser are somehow their fault. However, this is untrue. With abusers who "split," victims will constantly be functioning in high-stress environments, cycling between adrenaline and dopamine, never knowing what to expect.

Summary

- Idealization and devaluation are part of the "splitting" phases of abusers, and they include alternating between heaping praise and heaping criticism onto the victim.
- These phases are used to keep victims confused and controlled in the relationship.

In the next section, you will learn about cognitive dissonance and how it can stem from trauma bonding.

Section 2: Cognitive Dissonance and the Dangers of Trauma Bonding

We have already discussed at length how the trauma bond functions, but what makes a trauma bond *dangerous*? This is not a normal, healthy bond that we form in a safe environment; this is a bond that is wired within us before we can recognize it or fight back. In order to escape this toxic situation, victims have to fully understand the forces against them during this recovery. Many victims will know, deep down, how dangerous their bond to their abuser is, but it can be very difficult to see anything from an outside perspective while trapped in a toxic relationship. Being aware of the true dangers of the situation can help victims gain this perspective.

Some of the dangers of abusive relationships are physical if this is the type of abuse that the victim is subject to. You may see actual bruises on the skin and body of the victim. This is a clear danger, as those who are involved in a traumatic bond will return to their abuser even though the threat of physical danger is very real. Family members and friends may attempt to step in and stop the abuse. Their interference *can* be helpful, but depending on how strong the trauma bond is, the victim may simply isolate themselves from those friends and family members. Due to the cycle of abuse and the constant idealization and devaluation of the victim feelings can be so intense that the victim will subject themselves to the lows just for the chance of experiencing another high.

You may wonder what all this back and forth does to the human psyche. If the trauma bond is not resolved, then victims will find themselves constantly returning to their abuser. The average amount of times a victim will return to their abuser is seven, which is a strikingly high number—and this is the *average*, which means that the number could be even higher than this. It takes a long time to recognize and break a trauma bond.

If you are in one of these relationships, think about how many times you have forgiven your abuser, then about how many times you have left them only to return. This is nothing to be ashamed of, but it is something to be *aware* of. Cognitive dissonance and the trauma bond are connected in this way. Both are ways to survive a situation that is unhealthy and toxic to your physical and mental well-being. Therefore, as terrible as it is to be loyal to someone who causes real harm to you, your brain is wired to do just that in order to survive.

Cognitive dissonance refers to your mind's attempt to process two opposing beliefs. This can happen when we learn something that contradicts our worldview or everything that we know about a person in our lives. This intense feeling of anxiety causes a "freeze" response in the brain which leads to denial, which is one of the most basic psychological defense mechanisms. Denial allows us to stay in a false sense of security instead of facing the harsh and toxic reality of the relationship we are truly in.

Within an abusive relationship, there may be a part of you who truly knows what kind of person they are. You can see it from the outside and feel that there is something terribly wrong. However, there is another part of you that wants to believe in the good in them. It craves the love bombing stage and the idealization that comes along with your toxic connection. These times are few, but there is just enough of them to keep you locked in, feeling like a change may be possible.

Cognitive dissonance manifests as confusion in the relationship. You may jump back and forth between believing your abuser and not believing them, or between thinking they're the sweetest and then thinking they're hurtful. It's difficult to see the truth head-on, so our mind sprinkles in pieces of it at a time. This is where the denial comes in. For survival, you may choose to believe that your abuser is a good person who has a temper from time to time. This is a way to give yourself the security you've been craving in the relationship.

You will know that you're experiencing cognitive dissonance if you notice yourself going back and forth constantly. This may happen quietly in your thoughts or openly in conversations with friends and family. Many victims may even be out of the relationship for several years, but still feel a cognitive dissonance surrounding their abuser. This is because they likely weren't able to process and accept the true nature of their abuser. They will often experience loss of memory surrounding traumatic events within the relationship, or they may still debate mentally whether their abuser was "really that bad". This is the way our brain protects us from trauma.

The danger of cognitive dissonance is that it removes reality from your thoughts. You might find that this confusion begins translating into other aspects of your life, or that you spend all day trying to puzzle out your relationship, when deep inside you *know* it is harmful. In order to resolve cognitive dissonance, your abuser needs to be labeled for what they truly are and you must see the abuse for what it is. Until this happens, the feelings of uncertainty will continue. If you need help with this, a therapist can give you the tools to recognize your abuser's manipulation tactics, and friends and family can help you sort and validate your feelings.

Summary

- The dangers of trauma bonding can be both physical and mental.
- Cognitive dissonance happens when you try to believe two conflicting ideas at the same time. This can contribute to the confusion surrounding the true nature of an abuser.
- Cognitive dissonance is a coping mechanism used to deflect trauma, survive, and bond with the abuser.

In the next section, you will learn how Stockholm Syndrome keeps victims trapped in relationships with abusers.

Section 3: Stockholm Syndrome & Trauma Bonding in Narcissistic Relationships

In many trauma-bonded abusive relationships, the abuser exhibits behaviors that align with Narcissistic Personality Disorder (NPD). "Narcissist" has become a buzzword, often used to describe people who are full of themselves, but it's a genuine psychological term and mental illness. Individuals with NPD fall in love with a grandiose version of themselves to mask their extreme insecurities. While they may *appear* to be overly confident, deep inside, they are unsure of their abilities and are constantly comparing themselves to everyone around them. In order to deflect and ignore their true feelings, they engage in many dysfunctional behaviors.

These behaviors are often with regard to those around them. They can include a lack of empathy, a need for admiration, and an exaggerated sense of importance. People may view them as selfish and demanding, and their relationships often suffer due to it. Narcissists show a tendency to take out their inward feelings of anger on the people around them. Some other signs of narcissism include:

- They have a sense of entitlement.
- They expect to be recognized as superior, even if it isn't deserved.
- They monopolize conversations.
- They belittle those they see as inferior.
- They have difficulty recognizing the needs or wants of others.
- They react negatively to criticism.
- They manipulate those around them to get their way.
- They have difficulty regulating their emotions.
- They struggle with change, even when their behavior becomes a problem.

These behaviors can be difficult to handle for those closest to a narcissist. We now know that trauma bonding happens when there is a repeated cycle of abuse, which increases the need for validation and positive feelings; the same thing happens in a narcissistic relationship. When someone is struggling to please a narcissist, they may go through a cycle of abuse. This creates a strong trauma bond and feelings of guilt, leading them to believe that there is something wrong with the way *they* are behaving, rather than the narcissist.

Many narcissists also employ manipulation tactics that are used to form a trauma bond, including **gaslighting** and **projection**. Narcissists project their insecurities and anger on the victims. If you are in a romantic relationship with a narcissist, you may struggle to meet their expectations and prove that you are good enough for them. This is because many narcissists feel they aren't good enough, and they seek validation by making the people around them feel the same way. A romantic partner is perfect for this because there are so many feelings involved. These people tend to pick victims who are empathetic, understanding, and trustworthy. In essence, their partners are usually the opposite of them. Let's look at an example of how a narcissist may project onto their victim:

Example: George and Kayla have been together for about six months. Their relationship has been tumultuous and they have broken up several times because Kayla has caught George texting other women. However, they keep getting back together. Even though Kayla has shown no signs of infidelity, George is very suspicious of Kayla. A co-worker texts Kayla about a work matter after work, and George sees the message. He begins yelling and accusing her of doing something behind his back. Meanwhile, he is still texting other women in an inappropriate manner without Kayla's knowledge.

This is an example of projection. Oftentimes, when a narcissist accuses their victim of something without reasonable cause, they are doing the thing in question. Subconsciously, they may assume that everyone behaves the way they do, and to the narcissist, they will never be in the wrong. Therefore, they have to project their own issues onto others and blame them. This creates extremely toxic situations.

Trauma bonding in abusive relationships, *especially* narcissistic ones, has strong similarities to **Stockholm Syndrome**. This is when people who are held captive begin to have positive feelings toward their captures. The term originated in 1973 after there was an attempted bank robbery in the Swedish city of Stockholm. For six consecutive days, employees of this bank were held as hostages. Police were able to rescue the hostages on day seven. However, the hostages actually attempted to defend the robbers; they wouldn't give testimony against them, and they collected money between themselves to defend the robbers in court. This intense misalignment of trust only took a few days to develop.

This syndrome is often observed in POWs and victims of concentration camps. However, it isn't exclusive to captives; it is also observed between children and their abusive parents, and between parties in narcissistic relationships. However, as discussed in the article "Stockholm Syndrome and Trauma Bonding in Narcissistic Relationships"

(2020), while the victim doesn't need to be a *captive*, there are several conditions that must be present:

1. **There needs to be a perceived threat to the victim's life.** The victim's life doesn't need to be *physically* threatened; emotional and psychological threats to the victim's life, common in toxic and narcissistic relationships, can also fill this condition. For example, a narcissistic abuser may rage if they feel that they've been criticized, and even if they've never become physical before, the victim may feel unsafe during these situations. Even if the victim isn't consciously aware that they fear for their life, their body will still react to the traumatic situation. In the case of the Stockholm robbery, the victims were well aware of the threat, yet they were still able to sympathize with their captors. In a romantic relationship, there may be no "actual" threat, but that does not lessen the danger.

2. **The victim must be isolated from contact outside of their abuser.** In many toxic relationships, the victim is isolated from family and friends. This generally happens slowly, over time. The abuser will warp the victim's sense of self so that their primary goal is to appease their abuser, thus pulling the victim away from others in their life. When isolated, the victim may fail to notice how abusive their situation has become. This is how the abuser warps the victim's perception of their situation, forcing them to filter everything through the lens of their abuser. Without input from others, the trauma bond can strengthen, heightening the sympathy that the victim feels for the abuser.

3. **The victim must believe that they are incapable of escape.** The victim feels that they are unable to escape. It could be that the abuser directly tells the victim that they can't leave, or it may only be perceived out of fear. The tantrums of an abuser can make a victim worry about what the abuser is capable of. In the robbery of the Stockholm bank, one of the employees had the ability to escape, but they chose not to. They may have simply frozen out of fear, or they may have been afraid of what would happen if they tried to escape. In a romantic relationship, the victim may have reasons for being unable to leave, such as finances or their unwillingness to leave children behind. Either way, the victim

needs to feel that they cannot leave the relationship and that if they *tried* to, the detriments would outweigh the benefits.

4. **The victim must be shown some kindness.** For sympathy to form for the abuser, they must show some kindness to their victims. In a romantic relationship, we typically see this during the love-bombing stage. This is how the narcissist lures the victim in and tempts them to stay; after all, they're not *always* bad. For someone in a toxic situation, any ounce of kindness will be appreciated. If a victim is pushed to their limit and is willing to go through the pain of leaving to escape abuse, but their partner then switches back to the love bombing stage, it will seem much easier to the victim to stay and feel loved rather than to leave.

Stockholm Syndrome results from repeated abuse. When we are unable to survive using the typical "fight or flight" mechanism, this is another option. In the robbery at the Stockholm bank, the hostages could not fight or run from the armed robbers; they knew they could be shot if they tried. They were under extreme amounts of stress and had no ways to even try to protect themselves. This feeling of being trapped leaves the brain desperate to find security, forcing it to form bonds with the robbers.

Humans aren't built to handle stress long-term. It can have damaging physical and mental effects. This is why our brains may resort to denial and only looking at the positive. Those involved in the robbery may have instinctually sided with the robbers for survival. Many abuse victims do this as well, especially if they know that the abuser is prone to violence. They don't want to provoke them and "cause" harm, so instead, they walk on eggshells and try to appease them. However, this is no way to live; it only causes the victim to assume blame for the abuser's behavior.

From the outside, this coping mechanism may seem illogical to others. However, it's a way for the victim to cope with the ongoing abuse and try to diffuse toxic situations with their abuser. It might not make *sense*, but it is a biochemical response ingrained within the human brain. Those who haven't been in an abusive relationship may not understand how the victims could feel sympathy toward their abuser, but this is because they haven't experienced the chemical connections and survival responses of severe trauma.

Summary

- Narcissistic Personality Disorder (NPD) leads to feelings of grandiosity and an inability to empathize with other people.
- Many narcissists repeat a cycle of abuse toward their victims, causing them to feel trapped.
- Stockholm Syndrome makes the victim feel sympathy toward their abuser, and it can happen in abusive relationships.

In the next section, you will learn how PTSD plays a role in traumatic relationships.

Section 4: When Trauma Becomes Post-Traumatic Stress Disorder

Post-traumatic stress disorder (PTSD) happens after someone undergoes a traumatic event that greatly decreases their ability to function. PTSD occurs specifically after a trauma that greatly alters the way we perceive and react to the world around us. A tricky aspect of PTSD is that the time period between the trauma and the onset of symptoms varies widely; symptoms may show within one month, or they may take years. This means that, even if you have escaped the parent or partner that you were trauma-bonded to, you may still experience PTSD symptoms from your time with your abuser. These symptoms can cause significant problems in social and work situations. There are several symptoms to look out for:

- **Intrusive memories/thoughts.** You may have continuous and unwanted memories of your trauma. Even while you are at work, school, or with family, you may still be unable to focus on anything other than the specifics of what happened. Furthermore, you may have flashbacks of the traumatic event at the worst times. These intrusive thoughts can also manifest as dreams or nightmares in which you relive your trauma. These intrusions cause severe stress, and they can prevent the victim from moving on from their trauma. Though they may be physically away from the abuser, their mind is still trapped in the trauma of the situation, trying to comprehend what happened.

- **Avoidance.** Instead of dealing with the trauma, you may avoid it completely. People in your life may be concerned about what you went through, yet you have difficulty talking about it altogether. You may even avoid going out anymore or going to specific places that remind you of the traumatic event or the person who caused it. For victims, it is crucial for them to fully understand that what happened was *not* their fault. Talking to a therapist or another professional is how they will be able to process their trauma. If they just avoid it, it will be buried deeper inside and will come to the surface in unhealthy ways.

- **Negative changes in thoughts and emotions.** Before the traumatic event, you may have been a positive person, but now you feel poorly about yourself and the world around you. You might even have general hopelessness about the future. Trauma infects your memory; it can cause cognitive dissonance or confusion surrounding which beliefs are real. This can cloud your memory and make it difficult to remember what exactly happened. Many people with PTSD distance themselves from family and friends and lose interest in things they used to enjoy. They may even feel numb and be unable to experience pleasure and happiness toward the things that once made them feel most like themselves.

- **Changes in reactions.** Those with PTSD may be constantly on guard, which manifests in being easily startled and slow to trust. They may even rethink the relationships in their life and wonder if they can trust anyone at all. They may also engage in self-destructive behavior such as substance abuse. Everything we've listed contributes to trouble sleeping and concentrating, and causes irritability and outbursts of anger. Many victims even feel shame and take on the guilt of what happened to them, even though it is not their fault. Without processing what happened to them, the victims may feel that they should have been able to prevent it somehow.

There are many links between PTSD and abusive relationships. Many people who go through relationship violence end up experiencing symptoms of PTSD, and in addition to this, women who experienced abuse in childhood are more likely to experience violent romantic relationships in adulthood. It is a common misconception that PTSD is only found in veterans; PTSD is not exclusive to those who have been through intense combat. It's also important to recognize that not all people who suffer from PTSD will be violent or have anger outbursts.

In a trauma bond, there is constant trauma happening. The cycle of abuse continues and the victim may think that they are not experiencing traumatic events, but each abusive cycle brings another trauma. Each period of calm only brings another period of abuse. This is shocking to the nervous system and damaging to the psyche. Many victims of abuse will experience PTSD at some point, but it may take months or years for the symptoms to show.

The danger here with the trauma bond is that the victim will not leave. The toxicity involved in an emotionally abusive relationship may be more subtle. The victim might be willing to stay and forgive their partner for whatever they do, but this doesn't mean that the emotional trauma won't cause symptoms of PTSD. The continued abuse will only make the PTSD more severe, and can eventually cause **Complex PTSD** (C-PTSD).

C-PTSD is also the result of trauma, but it is caused by a long-lasting trauma rather than a relatively isolated traumatic incident. This type of PTSD forms when trauma lasts over a period of months or years. C-PTSD includes all of the symptoms of PTSD, but also includes the following:

- **Irregular emotions.** Many victims feel they have a rollercoaster of emotions throughout the day, feeling happy one moment and sad the next. This can be extreme, with some people suffering from anger outbursts or bouts of depression.

- **Low self-esteem.** Due to the trauma and abuse, the victim may have low self-esteem going forward in life. It may be difficult for them to feel confident, and they may feel they aren't as good as others. Their work life and social life can suffer because of this.

- **Difficulty forming relationships.** After enduring trauma at the hands of someone they trusted, the victim may have trouble forming relationships. They may not trust that other people have good intentions. Children who grow up in toxic situations may never learn what healthy attachments look and feel like, leaving them far more likely to enter unhealthy romantic relationships in adulthood.

- **Detachment from the trauma.** In an attempt to deal with the pain surrounding their trauma, many victims detach completely. They may disconnect from it and from the world around them in an attempt to forget what happened. Some victims have trouble remembering events fully, as their brain does this to protect them from the trauma.

- **Loss of self and meaning.** Many victims lose their sense of self, leading to feelings of uncertainty. They may feel that there isn't any meaning to their life, and they may feel trapped in the abusive time period. Children raised in a toxic environment may not have been able to cultivate their sense of self from a young age due to their environment.

Symptoms of C-PTSD are far more ingrained into the victim's psyche than normal PTSD symptoms. They can affect a person's work, social, and family life. Those who were raised in an abusive household without a method of processing their trauma are at severe risk of becoming functioning adults living with C-PTSD, and victims who were in a relationship with their abuser for many years may develop C-PTSD as well.

Summary

- Post-Traumatic Stress Disorder (PTSD) happens after someone experiences a traumatic experience in their life. It can show up anywhere from a month after to several years after the event.
- There are several symptoms that must be present in order for a person to be diagnosed with PTSD.
- Within a trauma bond, trauma is experienced over an extended period of time rather than all at once, putting the victims at risk of developing Complex PTSD (C-PTSD).

In the next section, you will learn how narcissists use intermittent reinforcement to get you addicted to them.

Section 5: How Narcissists Use Trauma Bonding & Intermittent Reinforcement

"If they're so bad, why didn't you just leave?"

So many abuse survivors hear this question, but the simple answer is the overwhelming influence of the trauma bond. When bonded with a narcissist, it's difficult to simply *leave*. Earlier we spoke about how narcissistic relationships can leave victims prone to Stockholm Syndrome, making them feel threatened, isolated, and trapped. In this section, we will discuss how abusers use intermittent reinforcement to make their victims feel trapped. This constant push and pull makes the victim feel that they are to blame for their abuser's moods when they are actually living in the false reality created by their abuser.

Intermittent reinforcement cycles between abuse and sprinkles of affection. This affection could be as small as a compliment or as large as a gift given sporadically throughout the abusive cycle. Let's look at an example of how this keeps the victim trapped:

Example: Last evening, Mark became furious at his wife Angela and slapped her across the face. She was hurt and shocked, so she decided to leave. She left the house and went to her friend's house for the night. Her friend told her that Mark's behavior is abnormal and extremely abusive. Angela decided that she was right and that she wouldn't take him back. However, when she came home in the morning, he was waiting for her with flowers. He told her that it would never happen again and that he only did it because he loves her so much. Angela thought that she was lucky to have someone who loves her so much, so she went back on her word and took him back.

In this situation, we see Mark being physically abusive to Angela. She takes the responsible steps to remove herself from the dangerous situation and go to a friend's house, but when she comes back, he is a completely different person. His claim that he only hit her because he loves her so much is obviously not true; abuse is not love. However, with their hormones running high and his quick switch to kindness, Angela decides to take him back. She is trauma-bonded to him, and the highs and lows become addictive. His promises are enticing, and her desperation to get back to the honeymoon phase is enough to make her return.

This intermittent reinforcement also creates a need for approval from the abuser. The victim hopes that the original mask the abuser had will return. The abuser may have been the person of the victim's dreams at the beginning of their relationship, which leaves the victim wondering where that person went. Because the positive aspects of the abuse are now so few, the victim gives them much more value than they should. This method of maximizing the minimal affection they receive while minimizing their abuse is a coping mechanism to give the victim hope and avoid dwelling on their danger.

Whenever we are in a threatening situation, we will look for any kind of hope that the situation could improve. All signs of kindness will be interpreted as proof that the abuser really isn't that bad. However, the abuser will not change. Many victims hold onto the belief that they can "change" their partner or parent, or that they can get better. Victims make excuses for their abusers' behavior, citing a bad childhood or other stressors. Especially with narcissists, it is extremely rare that their partner will be the reason they finally change. Narcissists have to make the conscious choice to be aware of their actions, take accountability, and get help from a professional, which is extremely difficult for them given the influences of their personality disorder. This is impossible for him for him to seek help from a professional because he has a strong belief of what he is.

There is also a biochemical element to the victim's thoughts. Much like a drug, the victim becomes addicted to the toxic nature of the relationship. As we discussed in earlier, when powerful hormones are involved, the abusive nature of the relationship actually strengthens the bond for the victim. Some examples of these hormones are oxytocin, dopamine, cortisol, and adrenaline. The victims mistake these intense reactions for an intense love for their partner, even though it is harmful and unhealthy.

There are many signs that your partner or parent may be using intermittent reinforcement against you. Here are some to look for:

1. **You know they're manipulative, yet you hold on.** Sometimes, we have a feeling that something within the relationship is terribly wrong. As we spoke about, you may cycle between loving and hating your abuser. However, a part of you is always aware of their true toxic nature. You might even ruminate over the abuse but only focus on the positives of the relationship when with others. Part of you wants to let go of them forever, but you can't bring yourself to do it. This back and forth is a clear sign that the abuser is using intermittent reinforcement. You

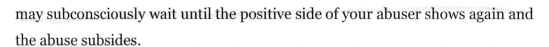

may subconsciously wait until the positive side of your abuser shows again and the abuse subsides.

2. **You walk on eggshells around the abuser.** Narcissistic abusers are known for raging over small things. This may cause you to be on edge around them, wondering when they will throw a tantrum next. This is no way to live around someone who is supposed to love you. You shouldn't have to worry and filter every word you say. However, victims of narcissistic abuse learn how to do just this. This keeps you in a constant state of uncertainty and creates feelings of danger, even if there isn't an immediate threat. Your adrenaline will be running high, and you will always be in a state of worry.

3. **You defend your abuser and keep the full truth to yourself.** You don't like telling people about the true nature of your relationship. You might only tell people the positive things they do for you during the cycle of abuse in order to stay in a state of denial. If some of them know what is happening and show concern, you may continue focusing on the positives to try to convince them that everything is fine. You will also defend actions that you can't prevent your family and friends from seeing, such as a bruise that they've already spotted before you could cover it. Often, abusers—*especially* narcissistic abusers—will be careful about how they act in front of other people. Much of the abuse happens behind closed doors, and your friends may be surprised to find out the true nature of the relationship. However, when a tantrum happens, the abuser may not be able to control themselves. If this happens in public, you won't be able to shield others from their true nature. Part of you may want to because you truly believe the narcissist is not "that bad", but this is due to denial.

4. **Even if you leave them, you believe their plans to get better.** If you leave a narcissistic abuser, they may reach out to you and try to get you back. They will love bomb you and promise to be better, and they'll suddenly turn into the person that they *know* you want them to be. In previous arguments, you may have expressed aspects of them that you didn't like and wanted them to change, and when you finally leave, they finally talk about those aspects of their behavior and

promise to correct them. Many victims fall for this, feeling relieved that their abuser finally sees the error in their ways. However, when you go back, things will be worse than ever; everything they said to get you back will be dismissed.

5. **You develop behaviors that are harmful to yourself.** You might self-harm or begin abusing substances in order to escape the reality of your situation. Many victims do this because they take on the blame for staying in the relationship and feel shame about their situation. If family members or friends put pressure on the victim to leave the relationship, it may add stress even if it is done out of love and concern. The only person who can decide to leave is the victim.

6. **You begin changing who you truly are inside.** Abusers pretend to love who you are at first, but over time, they try to change you into what they want. It's exhausting trying to meet their unrealistic expectations; when you're constantly put down by your abuser, your self-esteem diminishes until you no longer feel confident in who you are. As the cycle of abuse continues, you may fully give up and become what they want you to be. Once you do this, it becomes easier for narcissistic abusers to use intermittent reinforcement and chip away at anything you once loved about yourself.

If you recognize any of these in your own relationship, know that you are not alone. A relationship with a narcissistic abuser is insidious because, with each cycle, the abuse becomes worse. This is how emotionally or psychologically abusive relationships can escalate into physical abuse. If you are in this kind of a relationship, you are *not* stuck forever, and there are ways you can escape this situation. We will discuss ways you can break this trauma bond and take back your life in the next section.

Summary

- Narcissistic abusers use intermittent reinforcement, including abuse followed by kindness, to keep the victim mentally trapped in the relationship.

- If you are unsure whether your abuser uses intermittent reinforcement against you, consult the list of signs of intermittent reinforcement and think over whether you recognize them in your own relationship.
- When victims leave them, narcissistic abusers tend to promise to change, specifically in aspects that the victim has expressed distaste for in the past, to rope them back in. This is the "kindness" phase, but once the victim returns, the abuse will be worse.

In the next section, you will learn the steps to breaking out of a trauma bond.

| Part 4 | Winning & Breaking Free

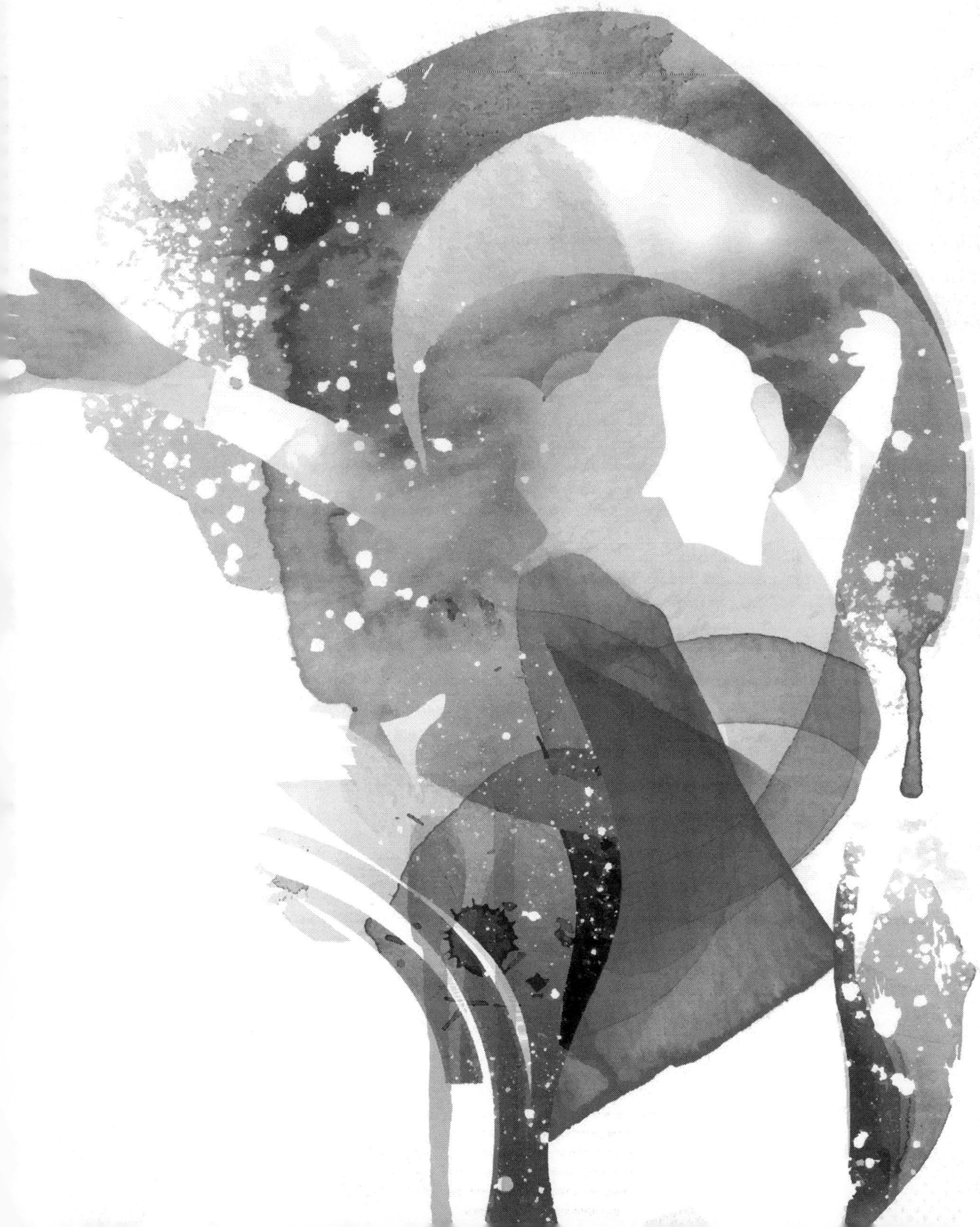

Section 1: Breaking the Trauma Bond

A trauma bond will not break overnight. It took time for this bond to form, and it will take just as much time, if not more, for it to break. We have to be patient with ourselves; we have to understand that what we've been through is not normal, and it has done damage to our mental and emotional health. In order to even think about breaking the trauma bond, we have to be in the right headspace. Ask yourself the following questions:

- Why do you want to break the trauma bond?
- Are you ready to live a life without abuse? Without fear?
- Do you want to leave behind your life of constant doubt and anxiety to begin a life filled with certainty and healthy relationships?
- Are you tired of sacrificing your life and well-being to please your abuser?
- Does a life filled with healthy connection and security sound better than the one you currently have?

Before we make any big change in our life, it's important to know why we are doing it. You have decided to break this trauma bond to improve your health. It is not possible to continue living in a trauma bond while also having a happy and fulfilled life. When you are ready to break this toxic connection, these are the steps you must take:

1. **Educate and examine.** By reading this book, you are taking the first step to end the trauma bond between you and your abuser. The more you understand the nature of your relationship and how this bond impacts your life, the more clearly you will be able to see. Educating yourself and reading up on the topic of abuse and toxic connection will help you recognize that there's nothing wrong with you as the victim, and it is not your fault that you ended up in this situation. Many victims feel that they should be better by now or should be over it when in reality there's much more to it. Psychology and biochemistry can keep us trapped, but having an awareness of this gives the power back to us.

2. **No contact.** In order to fully separate yourself from the trauma bond, you must cut off your abuser entirely. You might shudder at this thought, but unless you remove them from your life, you will not be able to stop the cycle of abuse that

has been created. It will be difficult—your body will go through withdrawal due to the hormones we've discussed, and you might crave them. However, after a few months, you will feel *much* more secure and calm. Your life without your abuser will be filled with much more positivity. There are some cases in which people can't go completely no-contact because of children, family, etc, but if you are in one of these situations, you still must go as minimal contact as possible. With the trauma bond, your abuser is in your mind already—having their constant texts or calls will *not* help you move forward.

3. **Focus on positive relationships.** To learn to form healthy attachments, you need to focus on creating safe and healthy bonds with other people. This could be family members or friends who you know want the best for you and who you can trust. You may even want to attend a support group for survivors or join a religious community. Making healthy friendships can create a way for you to see that your relationship was unhealthy. You may have a tough time relating or trusting others after your abusive relationship, but you can start small.

4. **Do things you love.** While in the relationship, you may have pushed aside activities you once loved to do. This is a great way to start small and begin trusting others again. If you love exercising, go back to the gym or start running again. Maybe join a class or go on a trip. Do something that interests you and stimulates your passions and goals. This helps rebuild your confidence and self-esteem after it was torn down by your abuser. This will also encourage the circulation of hormones that will help you stop dwelling over your trauma and help you move on.

5. **Talk to a professional.** While a support group can be helpful, you may need one-on-one support to sort through your trauma. There are so many ways that therapists can help with trauma—they can help you break out of the abused cycle of thinking and they can help stimulate the healing process. Professionals can give you techniques that typical family members or friends wouldn't be able to. There is nothing wrong with seeking help.

6. **Don't date.** After a toxic relationship, many victims jump back into dating

because they feel lonely and crave their abuser. Instead of dealing with these feelings in a healthy way, many fill that need with another relationship. However, you may be in a vulnerable state after your abusive relationship ends. This puts you at risk of falling into another codependent relationship, or a relationship with another abuser. Instead of dating, focus this time on doing things that help you connect to others in a healthy, non-romantic way. You can volunteer, go out with friends, or do something else that creates feelings of safe and healthy connection. Once you're strong and healed from your trauma bond, you can start dating again. Taking time to yourself will help you ensure that you can tell the difference between a positive partner and a negative one in the future, keeping you safe from further abuse.

However, you may be wondering how you *can* heal from your trauma bond. Will spending time with friends and family do it on its own? The short answer is no, but the long answer can be found in the next section.

Summary

- Trauma bonds take time to form, and they take time to break, as well.
- You must understand why you want to break this trauma bond in order to do it in a healthy and productive way.
- The six steps to breaking a trauma bond include educating yourself, going no-contact, focusing on positive relationships, doing things you love, talking to a professional, and avoiding the dating scene for a while.

In the next section, you will learn the ten steps to cleansing your body and mind after a trauma-bonded relationship.

Section 2: The Ten Steps to Recovery

It takes time to recover from a trauma bond. Throughout your toxic relationship, the abuser may have promised you a lot; they give you fleeting feelings of euphoria, and then they eat away at your very being. However, there is hope to recover from this. Earlier, we looked over the steps to breaking a trauma bond. However, how do we purge the bond from our mind and body in the aftermath? The relationship that victims have with their abusers is deeply ingrained, and they'll take more than a few self-care days to recover from. To completely cleanse your mind, you need to have a plan. Luckily for you, we have one laid out here. Here's the ten-step plan to ground yourself in the truth and begin cleansing yourself of your toxic connection with your abuser:

1. **Live in reality.** After the relationship ends, you might still wonder what could have been. This is *not* helpful—it will only keep you trapped and connected to your abuser. Remind yourself *why* you decided to break the trauma bond. Fantasizing about what could have been doesn't keep you based in reality. It will only keep you focused on the positive stages of the abuse cycle. Instead, try to remind yourself that the abuser will *not* change, and no matter how many times you go through the cycle, things will *not* get better if you return. When in an abusive relationship, you were certainly connected to a *type* of reality, but it was the abuser's version of reality. They cultivate an environment where you must behave a certain way, speak carefully as to not upset them, and cut off people who might interfere with their narrative of the world. It's time to pull yourself out of this crazy world and ground yourself in the truth.

2. **Live in the present.** Try not to worry about what could happen in the future. You may have a lot of thoughts surrounding what your abuser is doing, what you will do now without them, and how things are going to change once the trauma bond is broken. It's okay to acknowledge that leaving this relationship is scary! Being in an abusive relationship can become "comfortable" after a while. Many victims cite the familiarity of their abuse as one of the main reasons they stayed. Take time to notice what you're feeling right now, how your abuser makes you feel, and recognize that these feelings are your *present*. Recognize these emotions

and how they are affecting you now. Don't give power to the future and what *could* be. Instead, acknowledge the truth of your relationship *today*.

3. **One decision at a time.** When we begin making changes in a relationship, we can fall into all-or-nothing thinking. Don't tell yourself that things have to change overnight, or that you have to stop thinking about this person altogether at the drop of a hat. Not only is this unrealistic, but it puts stress on you to recover immediately. We want to be patient with ourselves and treat ourselves with the kindness that we didn't receive from our abusers. Instead, make one positive decision for yourself at a time. Can you decide to delete all the pictures of your abuser on your phone? Do this one day. Can you throw out letters or delete emails or texts that they may have sent to you? Do this the next day, or whenever you feel ready for it. Recovery is a process; being patient with yourself will make it easier for you.

4. **Self-care.** As you make these decisions one day at a time, *only* make decisions that will help you, not harm you. If you find yourself feeling down one day, don't berate yourself for it. Instead, treat yourself like you would a friend who was feeling this way. Would you talk down to a friend who was missing an ex or feeling depressed about a traumatic event? Remind yourself that you are loved. Do something that you enjoy to center yourself. Do you feel like watching Netflix all day and just relaxing? Then do it! Would you prefer to go out for a long run and get some endorphins in your system? That's great as well! There is no wrong answer; just take care of yourself.

5. **Allow yourself to feel.** In a toxic relationship, you may have repressed your emotions for so long that you no longer know how to feel them. Writing your emotions down can be a good tool here. After the trauma bond is broken, the emotions may come flooding in; it can be overwhelming to finally feel all of the anger, sadness, and hurt that you denied yourself during the relationship. Notice when you're feeling sad, notice when you're missing your abuser, notice when you're feeling angry about their actions. It's okay to feel these things. You don't have to repress them or pretend that you don't feel them anymore. Once you

allow yourself to feel these emotions, you can process them and move on.

6. **Grieve the relationship.** Anytime we have a breakup or lose someone in our lives, we have to grieve for them. Leaving a toxic relationship and breaking a trauma bond will be even more difficult than a "normal" break up due to its addictive nature. You have to honor the fact that it will be difficult, and that you're going to grieve. Grieving, no matter how terrible the person was to you, is completely okay. If others around you are struggling to understand why you are grieving your relationship, it may be a good idea to take a break from these people as well. During this time, you want to surround yourself *only* with people who support and understand the trauma you've endured.

7. **Understand the addiction.** Really think about what you're grieving; try to understand that while you may be addicted to this person, the perfect image you may have in your head is only an illusion. Maybe your partner convinced you that one day, you were going to get married and have children. Think about that promise—was it ever *really* going to happen? Is this someone that you would feel secure in a marriage with? Would you really want them to raise your children? This addiction you have toward the abuser is all based on illusion; the promises they may have made to you while trying to reconcile were all false. Coming to this realization can be extremely healing for victims in recovery. The abuser was never the person you thought they were. Victims often see their abusers in a flattering light, but as you heal from the relationship, it will be harder and harder to see why you ever thought positively of them.

8. **What will you tolerate in the future?** In this toxic relationship, you most likely tolerated things that were unhealthy and damaging. This likely didn't happen immediately, but slowly, over time, you started giving in to their demands and outbursts. Think about what boundaries you allowed to be crossed and compromised while in this relationship, and write down a list of things you will *not* tolerate in the future. Think about the things that are an absolute *no* for you. It might look something like this one:

> *I will not allow someone to speak down to me.*

I will not try to fix someone who doesn't want to help themselves.

It's not my job to meet someone else's unrealistic expectations.

I do not have to change who I am to please someone else.

Abuse is not love, and I will not tolerate it.

9. **Rebuild yourself.** As you process what happened, start dreaming about what you want. What are your passions? Who do you want to be? Maybe you want to go back to school, get a new job, or join a church. At the end of the day, you just need to start doing things that bring you happiness and help you focus on yourself, rather than what you've been through. You are a whole person on your own—you don't need a relationship to be fulfilled. Tapping into things you used to love can bring back your true self. For so long, you were focused on another person's wants and needs, and this can make you completely lose sight of what you love! This is the step where you can shift the focus away from "getting over" the abuser and focus on rekindling your relationship with yourself.

10. **Healthy connections.** Once you're feeling confident on your own again, you can start building connections with other healthy people. You don't want to jump into another codependent relationship or find toxic friends; build relationships that make you feel secure, bring you joy, and accept all the parts of you. We all need people and connections in our lives. Humans are social animals, and friendships can bring us so much happiness and peace. It's good to be vigilant when choosing friends and, eventually, romantic partners. Many victims will be wary when entering this phase, but it's something that should be celebrated!

Once you make it all the way to step ten, you can consider yourself free of the trauma bond—it is a long and arduous journey, but it will be so worth it once you get there.

Summary

- We have to go through a period of cleansing to heal from a trauma bond, just like we would from any other addiction.

- The ten steps to recovery are centered around focusing on yourself, staying grounded in reality, rediscovering your sense of self and your boundaries, and forming healthy relationships with people who care about you.

In the next section, you will learn how to get over a breakup with a narcissist, and what to look out for as they try to rekindle the cycle of abuse.

Section 3: How to Get Over a Narcissist

Ending a relationship with a narcissist may leave you with a lot of confusion. You know, deep down, that it wasn't your fault, and still harbor feelings of guilt. You know the relationship was abusive, but you felt so amazing during the love-bombing stage, and you can't forget the good times you had. If you're still stuck in the trauma bond, there are ways that you can work on getting over an abuser with narcissistic traits. These people have their own way of inflicting harm to the people they are supposed to care for in your life. Getting over a narcissist is similar to the way you would get over any abuser, but due to their specific nature, you may have to take additional steps. The following are methods for removing yourself from the abuser's mindset and gaining confidence in your decision to leave them:

1. **Acknowledge the abuse.** Narcissists have a way of diminishing your feelings by making everything about them—in fact, this is one of the most well-known symptoms of Narcissistic Personality Disorder (NPD). Therefore, you may have tried to acknowledge the abuse before, but your abuser either dismissed it or turned it back onto you. Because of this, many victims don't acknowledge their abuse for so long that denial becomes second nature. You might have a hard time setting aside excuses that you've used for so long, and you might still blame yourself or try to diminish it all together. This is understandable, but learning to identify the manipulation tactics of narcissists and spot them in your own treatment will help you see your abuser in a new light. This will help you look objectively at your partner's behavior and recognize how unhealthy it is.

2. **Set your boundaries.** As we spoke earlier, going no-contact is the best situation. This boundary puts protection in place for your emotional, mental, and physical health. With narcissistic abusers, boundaries are not allowed; they often see boundaries as a threat to their power and influence. You might feel tempted to reach out or respond to them, so it's good to have a plan for how you will deal with this. Narcissistic abusers are notorious for finding ways to get to you; they may even talk to your friends and slip in things that they know will get passed along to you. This is only damaging and upsetting during the recovery phase.

Many narcissists also use a tactic called the **smear campaign**, in which they tell mutual friends and associates lies about the relationship in an attempt to "smear" your reputation. This defamation is deeply upsetting and may tempt you to react, but this is exactly what they want you to do. They will try to paint you as the "bad guy" in the relationship, but your family, friends, and anyone who is of value to you will know the truth of what happened. If it becomes difficult to maintain the boundary you have set, try to keep in mind that you deserve space to heal. If you cannot cut them off completely, consider going **gray rock**. Gray rock is a technique for interacting with manipulative and abusive people; it involves not revealing any personal information about yourself and appearing uninterested in the conversation. You can come off exactly like a "rock." This can be useful for people who cannot avoid their abusers because of children or other involvements that they can't avoid. The abuser will inevitably attempt to provoke them or find information about their life, so going grey rock shows the narcissist that their manipulation tactics no longer have an impact on you. This will make them realize that they can't use you as their emotional punching bag any longer.

3. **Confusing emotions.** You must prepare for painful feelings. You may feel grief, anger, sadness, anxiety, paranoia, or nausea, and this is all completely normal. We've discussed that many victims grieve their relationship with their abuser, regardless of how much trauma was caused. The same applies in a narcissistic relationship. It's extremely difficult to move on and process the rollercoaster of emotions after a narcissistic and abusive relationship ends. If the abuser is slandering your name, moving on quickly, or doing other things to provoke you, this can also cause a wave of reactive emotions. You might be tempted to jump back into the relationship in order to end this, but this is the worst thing you could do. The negative impact caused by being with your abuser is far worse than anything you could experience outside of the relationship. Victims often have thoughts like "I'm not sure if I feel worse with or without him," but this is entirely due to the trauma bond. These victims feel withdrawal from the relationship and the emotions that flood in after a breakup can cause

confusion and trick them into thinking that things were better with their abuser. Toxic relationships cause a great deal of pain, and it's difficult to deal with these emotional experiences alone. If possible, tell those around you how you are feeling so they can be sensitive to the recovery you are going through.

4. **Do you like them?** Ask yourself this question right now: do you *like* your partner? This is a tool that many therapists use when helping victims through abusive narcissistic relationships. If you can say yes, then what is it that you like about your partner? What exactly do they do for you that makes you attracted to them? These can be hard questions to answer for some victims. The trauma bond is so strong that they believe they love them, but when they step back and look at their partner in an objective manner, they find nothing attractive about them. However, there is a toxic connection; even though they can't answer what it is about their partner that they love, they still feel a deep connection. If you feel that this resonates with you, try to keep in mind what it implies—you should feel attracted to your partner for many reasons. They should add to your life and support you, not tear you down.

5. **Reclaim yourself.** There are so many ways that we change in order to appease our abusers. Our very character becomes a shell of what it used to be in order to fit the abuser's needs. Maybe they told you they didn't like your clothes, so you changed your style, or they told you it was stupid to waste time going to the gym, so you stopped. Get back to the things that brought you joy and expressed who you were before the abuser took them from you; allow yourself to be not only who you *used* to be, but who you *truly* are. Often, the times when we feel like we don't want to be alone are the times when we actually should be. You will feel extremely lonely after the narcissistic relationship ends because it was all-consuming. It took over your whole life and entire sense of self. A narcissistic abusive relationship cannot function "properly" for the narcissist unless the victim gives up what is true to them, so when the relationship is finally over, you may feel lost for a little bit. This is the time to be alone and find yourself again. This will take time and it won't be easy, but reclaiming yourself will be liberating.

You will rediscover the things you used to be passionate about and finally live for yourself again.

6. **Lingering feelings.** Wouldn't it be great if we could just choose to stop loving someone? Sadly, this isn't possible. Even if someone causes us harm, we can't stop loving them immediately. You must understand that you don't have to stop loving someone in order to enter the recovery phase; in fact, if you try to wait until you don't love them anymore, you will only stall your healing. It can take a long time to stop loving someone, and there is nothing wrong with this! Your narcissistic abuser may be moving on quickly, and you may wonder why you can't. However, you must remember that a healthy person does *not* move on so quickly. True love doesn't function like this. You loved someone fully, and may still love them, and this is never anything to be ashamed of. You can continue loving them while recognizing that their behavior is abusive and unacceptable. As long as you recognize this, then the love you have for them doesn't matter. Accepting this can help you move on. Over time, you will notice how much happier and healthier you are without the person that you once devoted your life to.

7. **Self-care practices.** This is where small things will matter. Make sure you're getting enough sleep, eating well, relaxing, and using positive coping skills. You don't want to succumb to unhealthy coping mechanisms, such as substance abuse or other unhealthy relationships, to numb yourself to this one. Self-care techniques impact our mental health in a normal situation, but when we have the additional stress of dealing with a trauma bond, we have to put special emphasis on our self-care. This involves learning to say no to people and set boundaries. In an abusive and narcissistic relationship, you probably couldn't say no without the abuser being upset. This is because one symptom of NPD is a lack of boundaries; when they want something, they want it now, and they will not understand if you aren't able to provide that. Now that you're out of the relationship, you may find that you're not sure how to assert yourself anymore. That's okay—you can learn again. Start thinking things over before you do them. Is going to dinner at that

new restaurant with your friends something you *really* want to do, or would you rather stay home and get a good night of rest? Practice saying no and don't assume blame if your friends feel upset. You do *not* have to take responsibility for other people's feelings.

8. **Be patient.** The recovery time will be different for everyone. Don't compare yourself to other abuse victims; each situation is completely different, and everyone deals with trauma in their own way. Be patient with your mind and your body, and let yourself fully recover before jumping into anything else. Many victims of abuse may see other victims and wonder why they aren't as far or as happy as they are, but it's important to keep in mind that we never know what another person is going through. We can't know everything going through someone else's mind. Having patience with yourself will give you the time you need without the pressure of "getting better" as quickly as possible.

Summary

- Narcissistic abusers will try to lure you back into the relationship after you leave them; one technique they may use includes a smear campaign against you.
- Setting boundaries and either going no-contact or "gray rock" with the narcissistic abuser is the only way to keep their manipulation tactics from influencing you.
- Be patient with your recovery; each person takes their own time to heal from trauma and abuse.

In the next section, you will learn what happens when you go "cold turkey" from a trauma bond and the risks and benefits associated with doing so.

Section 4: "Going Cold Turkey"

Addictions to toxic relationships have been likened to addictions to drugs, in that they cause feelings of euphoria mixed with feelings of desperation. Those suffering from drug or alcohol addictions try many different methods to break the cycle of addiction; one such method is to completely cut out the addictive substance, which is referred to as "going cold turkey". Instead of weaning themselves off of the addictive substance, they abruptly stop their substance intake.

People may do this because they believe that it'll be easy to do, or because they assume that giving up the substance faster will break their addiction faster, or because they believe that they will only suffer through a short period of withdrawal. However, the discomfort caused by going cold turkey can be severe. Due to the abrupt stop, the body may have a negative physical reaction that can cause extreme pain and serious ailment. Many people underestimate how they will feel when they go cold turkey; in fact, sometimes it can lead someone to go back to the substance to get rid of the extreme agony they feel when giving up altogether. This is so painful for them due to the extreme dependency that they have developed.

There are physical and biochemical changes that happen in the body and brain when people form addictions through the regular use of an addictive substance. Your body learns to expect these substances and learns to rely on them for relief, which means that the body will react negatively if the substance is suddenly stopped.

These negative reactions are **withdrawal symptoms**; they are the body's way of trying to get the person to continue using the substance. Symptoms of withdrawal from substance abuse are similar to symptoms of withdrawal from a toxic relationship. Withdrawal from substance abuse can cause jumpiness, sweating, nausea, vomiting, loss of appetite, anxiety, depression, body aches, and other mental health issues. If you recall our discussion of Post-Traumatic Stress Disorder (PTSD), you may recognize that many of the above symptoms align with those associated with PTSD and breaking trauma bonds. These people experience anxiety, mental health problems, jumpiness, and other physical reactions to traumatic flashbacks.

Those who have abused drugs usually develop a tolerance to the substance, so over time, they have to take larger doses in order to get the same effect. They may start slow, but each time they use the drug, they need more to feel the effects. For a victim of abuse, the cycle creates a similar effect. The more times the victim goes back to the abuser, the more extreme the abuse gets. Therefore, if they leave the relationship abruptly, they will experience similar withdrawal symptoms as someone who has quit a drug cold turkey. There is a high risk that they will crave their abuser and return to the relationship.

However, after being free from the abuser for a while, they may not be accustomed to the level of abuse that they are about to experience. Similarly, someone who has attempted to quit a drug cold-turkey may return to the drug at the dosage they left off on. However, this can be very dangerous, as their body may no longer be accustomed to the high dosage; they run the risk of accidentally overdosing.

For those struggling with substance abuse, medically-supported detox is often recommended. This includes the assistance of addiction treatment professionals who can provide medications that will help with withdrawal symptoms and lower the likelihood of relapse. Inpatient and outpatient treatments are available. An inpatient facility would likely be a rehab center where the patient addict can stay during their treatment. This is a supportive environment in which the patients are weaned off of the drug and go through therapy to help them better understand their situation. The equivalent of this inpatient care for a victim of abuse would likely be a short stay in a mental health center. However, if this is not viable for the patient, there are support groups available, and there are ways that family members and friends can help to support the patient in this extremely difficult transition period. Victims of abuse can go to therapy to better understand their dependence on the abusive relationship and look through a more realistic lens at the trauma they have endured.

While going cold turkey is something that is not recommended for substance users, it is sadly something that victims of abuse *must* do. We know that victims return on an average of seven times, and we now know that this is likely because each time they find the courage to leave the relationship, they must go cold turkey. The urge to return to the abusive relationship can be extreme and even painful, and if the victim is not aware and armed with an understanding of the toxic connection at play, there is a strong chance that they will return to avoid the pain of withdrawal. There is no way to wean yourself off of an abusive relationship. The abuse either takes over your life fully or has no part in your life at all. Abusers, especially those with narcissistic tendencies, *need* their victims to be completely compliant and ready to give up everything about themselves. This is how they gain control. They will not allow a middle ground.

Going cold turkey is something that will be extremely difficult, but it is *necessary*. In order to move on from this toxic connection, you will have to cut the "substance"—in this case, your abuser—out of your life. However, just because you have to do this does *not* mean you have to do it alone. Arm yourself with knowledge so you can recognize your withdrawal symptoms and stay strong; just by reading this book, you've made tremendous progress in being able to do this. Whether you have left the toxic situation or not, you are arming yourself with the necessary tools and techniques to fight back against the trauma bond that has kept you in an abusive situation. Seek out people you can trust and allow them to support you throughout your recovery. Take help when it is offered by a trusted source, and ask for help when you need it. You will get through this.

Summary

- "Going cold turkey" refers to completely stopping the intake of an addictive substance to end an addiction, rather than weaning yourself off of the substance. This

- While going cold turkey is not recommended for people struggling with substance abuse, it is, unfortunately, the only option for abuse victims who are addicted to their abusers. Abuse victims cannot live a healthy life with abuse. They will experience similar withdrawal symptoms as those associated with drugs or alcohol.

- Allow friends and family to support you throughout your withdrawal from your abuser. Ask for help when you need it.

In the next section, you will learn how to overcome your trauma bond and heal from it for good.

Section 5: How to Overcome, Recover, & Heal

As we know from previous sections, trauma bonding takes a great deal of time to overcome. You can be consciously aware that someone is bad for you, and yet still miss them, but many victims feel shame because of this. They assume that they should just be over it already.

However, missing your abuser does not mean you cannot be "over it". To "overcome" something means that we have to be able to push through it, regardless of the obstacles in our way; in this sense, as long as you are able to handle missing your abuser and live your life functionally and healthily despite these feelings, you can consider yourself "over it". This is an important distinction; rather than "overcoming" meaning "feeling nothing about your past", overcoming means *perseverance*. Human beings are constantly persevering. Life isn't easy, and no one said it would be! When we are dealing with trauma bonds, we are definitely going through a tough time. You're working on overcoming a toxic and unhealthy connection to a person who never truly had your best interests in mind. All you have to focus on is getting through it.

As we discussed in a previous section, withdrawals from a trauma bond are comparable to withdrawals from alcohol or drugs. People struggling with such addictions are often told to take their recovery "one day at a time." Remind yourself to take things one day at a time when moving on from the abusive nature of your relationship. Even thinking about things in terms of a full day can be overwhelming when the trauma bond is first being broken; if this is too much, try taking it one hour, one minute, or even one second at a time. There is no wrong way to go about persevering through the pain. A trauma bond takes over your life completely, so when you give it up for good, you will feel it missing. However, you will eventually be able to build up momentum, and you'll start feeling better day by day.

As for your recovery, this can only begin once your motivation to persevere is in full effect. If you are not in the right mindset to push yourself through the tough days, tough hours, and tough minutes, then recovery simply isn't going to happen—and that's *okay*. You might spend the first few weeks or even months crying yourself to sleep at night and lingering in bed. The severing of a trauma bond can be a traumatic experience within itself, as it harshly jars both the body and mind. Because this trauma bond is so intense and emotional, it often affects all areas of life. Many victims have reported losing jobs, other relationships in their lives, and more. You will eventually need to take back control of your own recovery. Let's look at an example of how this could manifest:

Since breaking the trauma bond with her abuser, Kate hasn't been able to go out to eat at restaurants with friends or other people that she knows she can trust. For Kate, the voice of her inner critic still sounds like the voice of her abuser, and while she tries to do things she enjoyed before the relationship—such as going out with her friends—the voice of her abuser echoes in her mind. This is hard for her because all around her, she can see happy people enjoying their time together, and she wishes she could enjoy herself, too. It reminds her of things she used to do with her abuser that she can no longer do. However, after a long talk with her best friend, she is trying not to compare her journey to anyone else's. She is trying to remember that she can't see what's going on in someone else's life and that she never really knows what another person is going through. She knows that she can make assumptions based on how they act or the things they say, but everyone has their own inner life and inner critic.

So, if you've been struggling to eat at restaurants, your recovery begins when you *persevere* through this feeling. When you finally do go out the first time, it might not be great. It will take time to feel normal doing the things you once loved before the trauma bond. Many victims have talked about wanting desperately to get back to who they were before they met their abuser; they wish they could go back in time and never meet them.

This is where looking at things through a fresh lens can be helpful. Of course, this relationship was toxic and unhealthy, but you learned something, didn't you? And now, in recovery, you can decide what you want, and more importantly, what you *don't* want for the future. Breaking this toxic connection has helped you learn to be stronger. Now, this is where the healing process comes in, and a large portion of healing is simply understanding and having grace for yourself. When we can understand *why* we went through a tough time, we can better process the experience so we can move on.

At the end of the day, this was a traumatic experience that you lived through, but an experience that you can learn from nonetheless. You persevered and you're now on your way to recovery. You will be able to recognize this type of toxic connection forming in relationships going forward. This knowledge will help you heal something inside of you and allow you to move on from this toxic connection.

Summary

- Many victims wonder why they just can't "get over" their trauma bond because they assume that missing their abuser means that they haven't yet overcome them.
- The act of overcoming the trauma bond doesn't mean not missing your abuser, it means persevering through those feelings of loneliness and continuing on regardless.
- Once we learn to persevere, we can begin to recover and heal. We must take this process one day at a time.

In the next section, you will learn what signs to look for after you end a trauma bond that may mean it's time to ask for help.

Section 6: When to Ask for Help

Hopefully, after you end the trauma bond, you'll be able to move on with your life. It will take time and you'll have to be patient with yourself during the recovery. This process is when you will learn to be your own best friend, as there will be people around you who simply won't understand. Many people have never been through a situation like this, and some may judge you and be unable to understand where you're coming from. This is why you have to prepare for negative reactions. For victims in recovery, this can be harmful, as negative reactions can prevent them from moving on from the experience. This is why, as we've discussed, it's crucial to have *only* positive, encouraging, and supportive people around you.

If things just aren't getting better, mental health plays a huge role here. If you deal with mental illnesses such as anxiety, depression, bipolar disorder, or other personality disorders, you may be at higher risk for going into a deeper negative mental state after the relationship ends. This is always a possibility after any kind of relationship is over, but this is especially true with the trauma bond; we know that it's not just a *normal* breakup. These breakups are extremely intense and create grief comparable to if your partner had actually died. If this progresses to a certain point, you *need* to reach out for help. Here are some signs that it may be time:

1. **Constant anxiety.** It's natural to have anxiety after the relationship ends. You may be worrying about what your abuser is doing and thinking, or worrying about running into them. However, the anxiety should not last for months or years after the relationship, and it should not prevent you from going about your life in a functional manner. If you find that you are distracted from your life by lingering thoughts surrounding the relationship, or that you are unable to focus on anything besides your nervousness surrounding the trauma bond, then it might be time to reach out for help. Mental health professionals can give you crucial tools that are helpful with managing this overwhelming anxiety. This can include anxiety medications or various types of therapy, including but not limited to Cognitive Behavior Therapy (CBT). CBT challenges automatic thoughts and behaviors and works to replace them with more positive ones.

2. **Insomnia & Trouble Falling Asleep.** Again, this is a natural symptom of the

end of a trauma bond. Many victims struggle to sleep as the emotional effects of the abuse linger and creep in late at night. Similar to anxiety, however, this should not occur for months or years after the breakup, either. We need sleep for our minds to function properly. When we don't get proper sleep, everything can feel more overwhelming. This makes the intense emotions we are already dealing with feel much worse. If you haven't been able to sleep for weeks, it's definitely time to talk to your doctor.

3. **Feelings of Sadness and Hopelessness.** Feeling sad is bound to happen. You will be thrown off from your usual equilibrium, but like the above, this should not continue for months or years. It also shouldn't be so prevalent that you're unable to stop feeling hopeless. Hopeless feelings can be a sign of depression, which is a sure sign that you need to reach out for help.

4. **Difficulty with Relationships.** Many victims struggle to maintain relationships after leaving a trauma bond. This could even be relationships with close family and friends who truly care for them. However, trauma bonds can change the way that victims view the world and the people closest to them. Their abuser was someone they trusted, and it is upsetting to realize that a person you thought you could trust turned out to be so toxic and harmful. Not only this, but many victims will struggle to let new people into their lives going forward. You may find that you are hesitant to make friends or enter new relationships. This is something we will specifically talk about in later. It's crucial to be sure you are *completely* healed before entering a new romantic relationship after a trauma bond.

Something to note about the above symptoms is how long they last. You *will* feel different and not quite like yourself for a while. However, these symptoms become a cause for serious concern when they are persistent to the point that you are unable to participate in daily life. Many victims have reported that, at first, it was hard to think about anything else. This is because your mind will be trying to find the answers to everything that happened. However, this dwelling can quickly become a toxic cycle within itself and keep you trapped in the memory of abuse.

Therapy can be a great tool, even if you're not yet at the point when you can't stop the negative feelings. Sometimes, entering therapy immediately once the trauma bond has been broken can stop the negative cycle of dwelling and ruminating before it even begins. This can also help you navigate confusing thoughts as they arise in your recovery journey.

A great deal of pain that victims feel surrounding the end of a trauma bond is due to a lack of understanding. A great place to start is by reading and educating yourself with material such as this book! However, speaking with professionals and support groups filled with other people who have already been through the same thing can help open your eyes to the reality of your situation and why you are still stuck in the past.

Summary

- Pre-existing mental health problems are a risk factor in having a particularly severe recovery process after breaking a trauma bond.
- If you recognize any of the four listed symptoms in yourself, it is time to ask for professional help.
- Many victims struggle to move on because they are dwelling and ruminating on the trauma bond, trying to understand what happened.

In the next section, you will learn why it is important to put a hold on dating immediately following a trauma bond.

Section 7: Dating After Trauma Bonding

If you're just leaving an abusive relationship, then you are in a vulnerable place. Your whole world has been turned upside down. You have dealt with abuse and a toxic trauma bond to someone who did not care about your well-being and caused you harm. This will certainly have an impact on how you approach dating in the future. This can make dating *super stressful.* This is why it's important to make sure you are emotionally ready before entering a new relationship. There is no "right time" to start dating again; you don't need to follow anyone else's schedule. You want to have your confidence and sense of self back! This is what will help you be certain that the new bond you are forming is a healthy one and not a toxic connection.

When you first begin dating again, it can be difficult to connect emotionally. You will have your guard up and feel uncertain about trusting someone. During your recovery and healing phase, you may have gone back through your memory and recognized red flags from your abusive relationship that were there from the beginning. However, this is not something to punish yourself for; at this point, it doesn't matter that you didn't recognize them then. What matters is that you can recognize them now.

If you are not sure whether you are emotionally ready, here are some steps you can take to start a new chapter of your life after the recovery process is completed:

1. **Think about Healing.** getting help after the end of an abusive relationship can ensure that you are ready for something new. Taking the time to overcome, recover, and heal from the trauma-bonded relationship will ensure that your old emotions are not subconsciously affecting any new relationship you engage in.

2. **Take it Slow.** When you engage in a new relationship, go slow. There is no rush, no timeline. In your abusive relationship, everything might have been rushed, but this is only because your abuser wanted to trap you as quickly as possible. In a healthy relationship, this would not happen. Your new partner should respect that you need to take your time. If they cannot do this, then they may not be the right person for you.

3. **Trust Your Instincts.** After an abusive relationship, you might struggle to trust yourself, but this is the exact time when you need to. With your previous partner,

you likely recognized a great deal of red flags and simply ignored them because you didn't want them to be true. You likely did this because you loved your partner and wanted them to care for you in the same way. Therefore, you forgave them for many things that you likely shouldn't have, even things that were unforgivable. However, when you get that negative gut feeling now, the one that warns you that things are going wrong, be sure to listen to it. Do not be afraid to end a relationship or date based on this feeling alone. Remember: you do not owe anyone anything.

4. **Put Yourself first.** As you start dating, do not let the other person's needs and wants become a priority. You already did this in the abusive relationship, and it did not work. If your new partner is looking for you to do this again, then they are likely not a healthy option for a partner. Remember the self-care that you did after breaking the trauma bond; this self-care has to continue throughout your life now. It is *not* a one-and-done thing. Do not allow a new relationship to prevent you from living the life you deserve.

Despite being overly cautious and searching for red flags, you may still be experiencing residual symptoms from the abusive relationship. Many abuse victims have reported trouble functioning in a healthy relationship after being in such a chaotic environment for so long. They may simply not know how to function in a healthy way. Some even reenact situations or try to stir up fights because it is all they know. This is called **transference**, and it happens when the victim associates their new partner with the old one. They may react to situations as they would in the past relationship, or they may assume their new partner will hurt them in similar ways as the old one. This is definitely something to be aware of as you navigate the new world of dating. Your new partner should be someone you can *trust* and be *open* with. Tell them how you are feeling and let them know that there may still be some residual symptoms from the toxic environment you endured.

Summary

- Dating after a trauma bonding experience can be a terrifying idea.

- Do not try to date too soon; you want to ensure that you are fully recovered, mentally *and* emotionally, before entering into a new partnership. You need to be whole first.
- Practice your self-care, take your time, and remember to trust your gut instincts when dating someone new.

In the next section, you will learn about specific examples and case studies of trauma-bonded situations.

Section 8: Case Studies & Examples

Many victims feel embarrassed when they are trauma-bonded, and they may even feel embarrassed about their abusive relationship in general. This is born out of fear of what other people may think about them. They may worry that people will wonder why they stay, even though their partner is clearly bad for them. However, it's important to remember that it's not the victim's fault. This can be difficult for the victim to internalize since everything in the relationship has always been blamed on them.

Understanding just how common abusive relationships are can help you put this into perspective. Recognize that you are not the only one who has dealt with this before. It is upsetting just how often people are enduring abuse. Many endure this for years without even knowing because they've never been shown anything different.

According to the National Coalition Against Domestic Violence:

- Nearly 20 people per minute are abused by an intimate partner in the United States of America, which equates to more than 10 million people per year.
- 1 in 4 women and 1 in 9 men experience physical violence, sexual violence, or other contact violence that results in a series injury.
- There are over 20,000 phone calls a day to domestic violence hotlines all over the nation.
- 15% of all crime is due to domestic violence.

According to Social Solutions 2018:

- Nearly half of all women in the US experience psychological abuse by a partner at some point during their life.
- Most cases of domestic violence are not reported to the police.
- Men are less likely to report if they are subject to abuse.
- 5 million children are exposed to domestic violence every year.

These are shocking numbers; it is sad to know how many people are impacted daily, but it should also tell you that *you are not alone*. So many people experience this and have to deal with this same kind of hell that you are finding your way through, and you should not be ashamed of it. You are strong for finding a way out.

These types of numbers do have shocking consequences, both physically and mentally. Let's look at some of the possible effects:

- There is a strong connection between violence in a relationship and depression or suicidal behavior.
- Reproductive health problems are linked to partner violence. This could include stillbirth, miscarriage, abdominal pain, nutritional deficiency, chronic pain, anxiety, PTSD, cancer, and more.
- Domestic violence victims are at high risk for addiction.

Now that we have looked at the statistics and just how many people are affected by abusive situations within what is supposed to be a loving relationship, we can look at a specific example of how quickly a relationship can sour. Of course, not all relationships will turn bad this way. However, this can give you the tools you need to look out for early signs and protect yourself from falling in love with someone who only has bad intentions for you.

David and Mikayla have been together for five years. They met at a bar while Mikayla was out with her friends for dinner and David was with his friend grabbing drinks. They made eye contact, and as Mikayla recalls it, it was love at first sight. David asked for her number on the way out.

They went out for coffee a few times, and David mostly asked questions about her. Some of the questions were very personal right off the bad. He wanted to know things about her friends, her work, and her past relationships. She told him that she is still good friends with most of her exes, as they had amicable breakups. She asks about him, and he says that he doesn't speak to his exes anymore, but he doesn't have many.

After a couple of months, they start doing everything together. Mikayla tells her friends that David is the man of her dreams. He is handsome, funny, and charming in public. He makes her breakfast every morning, surprises her with gifts, and always calls her to check-in. They spend several nights per week together, and she feels herself growing deeply attached to him. David likes to hang out with her as much as possible, but because of this, Mikayla hasn't seen her friends in a while. She notices that David doesn't have many friends and rarely goes out. He only seems to have the one friend that he was with the night she met him.

Some of her friends are going out on a Saturday night and one of her exes will be there. She invites David, but he throws a tantrum and they have their first fight. He accuses her of cheating, saying that she only wants to go because her ex will be there. So, to prove her love for David, she cancels on her friends. Her friends are upset, but they say they understand, and they make a new date to hang out together. However, when the new date comes around, David again throws a fit, saying he doesn't want her to go. Mikayla assures him that her ex won't be there, but he tells her that he doesn't believe her.

After several months, Mikayla still hasn't seen her friends, and she only hangs out with David. Her friends stop contacting her because they know she won't come out, anyways.

David asks Mikayla to move in with him, and she agrees. However, her family is concerned and tells her that they never get to see her anymore. They tell her that they don't like David because he is isolating her. She tells them that she is just in love. David gets upset when Mikayla tells them what her family said, and he accuses her of not sticking up for him. She assures him that she told them that she is in love, but he tells her that "she should change their opinions." This makes her confused and upset because she is unable to change their opinion. So, instead, she stops talking to her family.

After a few more months, David tells Mikayla that he wants to have a baby. She tells him that she would prefer to get married first and wait a few years to do so. He throws a fit, accusing her of "not being committed to him." So they have a baby. Mikayla's family rarely gets to see the baby, and when they do, David hovers around, keeping a close eye on them.

Late at night, Mikayla notices David's phone has been buzzing. She finds out that he has been messaging with one of his exes on Facebook. She confronts him, and he claims that he is just friends with her. She recounts the time that he told her he was not friends with his exes, and he tells her that he "never said that." She begins to wonder if she is remembering incorrectly.

After a few weeks, she is still upset, feeling suspicious every time he is on the phone. When she brings it up again, he gets furious and slaps her across the face. Mikayla is shocked. She doesn't say anything again for several days, and then she decides to call her family and finally tell them what has been going on.

This situation is very common. Things always start out good, then slowly become sinister. Hopefully, Mikayla is able to get out and get help from her family. However, as we've discussed, abuse victims return an average of seven times. It would not be uncommon for Mikayla to leave, then for David to reach out to her, promise to change, and for her to return.

Recognizing negative signs early on can protect you from this happening. One red flag was when David asked such personal questions so early on. While there's nothing wrong with getting to know someone, there was no need for him to know such intimate details about her within the first few dates. When you are getting to know someone and just casually dating, it's good to take things slowly and be on alert for possible signs that they do have negative intent for you. The next red flag was that David became angered about Mikayla going out.

Any kind of romantic relationship should complement your life, not add stress to it. Many abuse victims report being constantly stressed and feeling anxiety toward things that are supposed to be positive and enjoyable, such as seeing family and friends. This is because they know their partner will react negatively to them being away.

David quickly continued to isolate Mikayla, after conditioning her into understanding that he had a fear of her going back to an ex. He used information that he probed for in their first few dates and threw it back in her face. Next, the two moved in together and had a baby. He had no respect for Mikayla's wishes. He ignored her timeline, manipulating her by accusing her of being uncommitted even though she was the one giving up everything for the relationship.

Ultimately, this led to a physical altercation. While these situations do not always turn physical, emotional abuse can have negative physical effects on the victim's body and mind over time. If you were never exposed to this kind of situation before, then you may have been unprepared to recognize these signs. However, you can now use this example to see red flags as they appear when you begin dating someone new.

Summary

- The statistics surrounding domestic violence and abuse in intimate partner relationships are much higher than expected.

- There is no shame in overcoming an abusive relationship. Do not feel embarrassed for having stayed so long. Instead, focus on celebrating your escape.
- Use the above example to see how quickly things can go wrong in an abusive relationship.

In the next section, we will address common questions that people ask about trauma bonds and what comes after them.

Frequently Asked Questions & Answers

Trauma bonding is an incredibly complex and traumatic experience. It can be shocking and jarring when we finally understand that we have come to be addicted to a person who has caused us so much pain. We have to accept that while we feel intense emotion toward them, they are no longer a good person to keep in our lives.

There are many questions that victims have surrounding these situations, and having questions is a good thing! Asking questions will help you better understand the situation you had to endure. We want to have a general understanding so that our minds can begin processing the situation and then moving on from it. However, it's important to note that focusing too hard on the "why" is not useful. People who are toxic and abusive in nature are not grounded in reality. They do not see or feel things the same way we do, so there usually isn't a "why" to their actions or to the abuse they inflict. Trying to assign reason and logic to an unreasonable person is a fruitless endeavor. In the end, it will only leave you feeling more confused than you were when you started.

So, let's take a look at some of the most common questions people have after they realize their partner was toxic, abusive, and they come to find that they were trauma-bonded to them all this time. We'll discuss the answers to these questions, and once we do, try to free yourself of them. Don't spend hours dwelling on them every day. You have already been through enough; it's your time to heal.

Question: Was it my fault?

Answer: Absolutely not! This is the most commonly asked question for all kinds of abuse victims. Even after leaving the toxic relationship, most victims still blame themselves for an array of reasons. They may still hear the abuser's voice ringing around in their mind. It can be difficult to get rid of this automatic response that they received from their abuser. Now that it has ended, it's only natural for the victim to assume, like most things in the relationship, that the blame would be assigned to them. Alternatively, the victim may blame themselves for not seeing it sooner. However, the quick and honest answer to this question is always *no, this was not your fault.* There is no way to see this coming! Many toxic people are master manipulators, and they know what to say and how to trap you. Do *not* blame yourself for fully loving another person. This is a positive trait you have: you have the ability to care for someone and love them, putting their needs above your own. This is something the abuser will never be able to do. They will never love someone truly in the way that you can.

Question: "Will I love them forever?"

Answer: There's no simple answer to this question, but it's important to remember that the relationship you had with this person was not based on honest and genuine love. While this may sting, it's the truth that you need to hear. This was more of an obsession, an addiction to something harmful. The more that this person denied you basic compassion, the more you tried to get it from them. This created a bond that made you believe you couldn't live without them. True love would never do this. Therefore, you may feel an intense emotion toward this person for a long time. However, over time, the feelings you have toward them will dissipate. As you encounter more positive people and places, you'll realize just how unhealthy this person was.

Question: "What if they find someone else and forget about me?"

Answer: The answer to this question is a bit of tough love, but they're going to do that. They've done this before you and they'll do it again after you. This may hurt, but remember that they will never have a relationship that is healthy or positive. They will continue to leave a trail of broken hearts behind them. They will never be satisfied in a relationship unless they are causing pain.

Question: "But they look happier than me. Are they?"

Answer: No and no. This is why, especially right after the relationship ends, it's important to go no-contact for a while and let yourself heal. It will be difficult to watch them as they go about their life pretending that they didn't cause the damage they did. Narcissists like to use social media platforms to get to you because they know you will be hurting. Make a vow to yourself to not let them. They no longer control you! It will take some time to get used to this feeling. Also, remember what it was like at the worst times. If you can keep a journal, write down all the things that they said to you in detail. Remember all the terrible things that you've pushed to the back of your mind in order to stay in the relationship. Read these when you are feeling weak, heartbroken, and wondering if they are having a better time with their new person or out with their friends. Open up that notebook and remind yourself that they are not happy; they are *miserable* inside, and they're just repeating these things over and over again to someone new.

Question: "When will I feel better?"

Answer: Everyone takes a different amount of time to heal. Some people have reported feeling better in a few months, a year, or even a few years. While, right now, that may seem like so much time, it really does begin flying by when you are living your life without this person. The more you live without them, and the more you realize you *can* live without them, the quicker you'll feel better. Life's possibilities and opportunistic doors will start swinging open once you no longer have this toxic weight carrying you down.

Question: "How do I avoid this in the future?"

Answer: Give yourself time. This is the easiest answer. Some people jump right back into relationships immediately, but this is dangerous because they may subconsciously be looking for traits that remind them of their abuser, which will lead them to fall into a relationship with another abuser. This usually happens out of a search for comfort and familiarity, and a longing to have their old partner back. If you give yourself time, you'll be able to recognize and avoid these signs in other people, further protecting yourself from this happening again. Remember that as you recover from this, you will also become stronger. The things we deal with, struggle through, and eventually overcome in life only make us more ready to take on things in the future. Life will continue throwing challenges at us and situations that we could never have foreseen. While you probably never saw this situation coming for you, you have made it through nonetheless. There will be other curveballs like this in the future, but just remember that you made it through this and you will be stronger and more capable with each coming day.

Summary

- Many victims are left feeling confused and hurt after suffering through an abusive relationship and the effects of a trauma bond.
- Do not look too hard for the "why", as there is no way to assign logic to an illogical situation.
- Be kind to yourself, and as time passes, you will discover how much stronger you are after living through this experience.

Conclusion

It takes a long, long time to understand a trauma bond. If you still feel attached to someone who has caused you serious harm in any way, whether physically, mentally, or emotionally, do not feel shame for that attachment. Shame and guilt are the *last* things you should be assigning to yourself right now because that attachment is not your fault. Instead, give yourself the compassion, love, and forgiveness that you gave to your abuser for so long.

Trauma bonding is a specific kind of attachment harbored between victims and abusers. It is not a positive bond—rather the opposite. These bonds trap victims in a cyclical state of abuse. We discussed one of the most familiar types, Stockholm Syndrome, which usually refers to those in captivity. However, it can also be applied to people in romantic relationships and to children with abusive parents. In order for Stockholm Syndrome to be present, there needs to be abuse, kindness, isolation, and a perceived threat of violence if there is an attempt to leave.

After the end of an abusive and trauma-bonded relationship, there are sure to be a lot of emotions. Before reading this book, you may have been unsure whether or not you were truly trauma-bonded to the person, or if you were just experiencing "normal" breakup feelings. However, something to remember is that within a toxic relationship, there is no normal. The reality you were living in was painful and unhealthy. While it is normal to form attachments to another human being, forming these attachments to a toxic abuser can keep you trapped in a cycle of abuse. Trauma bonding can form in many situations, such as domestic or child abuse, incest, or other exploitative situations.

There are many possible symptoms of being in a trauma bond, and they are both physical and mental. Many of the symptoms you may be having in your life can be related to the toxic nature of the trauma bond, even if you have no knowledge of it. One of the most common symptoms of being in a trauma bond is a constant feeling of anxiety about the relationship and about upsetting your abuser. It might feel like you are walking on eggshells around them, never knowing what will set them off. Or, if you do know what will set them off, then you are hyper-vigilant of it at all times. Another common symptom of a trauma bond is that when they act abusive, you make excuses for them and feel responsible for their behavior. Despite all of this, you still hold a strong feeling of addiction to them, regardless of what they do to you. Low self-esteem is another common feeling. This is due to the constant berating you may endure at their abuse. Lastly, but certainly not least, you will have an overall feeling of being unable to trust yourself or your perceptions of the world. A trauma bond is an unexplainable and obsessive addiction to something, one that you know, on a subconscious level, is not good for you.

Your partner uses a cycle of abuse in order to keep you trapped. This way, they are not *constantly* inflicting pain on you. They pepper in moments of affection to keep you hooked. The relative lack of affection makes the love stage feel more intense, and it releases chemicals and hormones in your body that strengthen your addiction to them. These stages include love bombing, in which they are outpouring love and affection, followed by an abusive event, in which you no longer recognize them and crave the love back. They will usually apologize profusely after this, swearing to change and promising that the relationship will be better than ever. Next will come a calm, and things will seem to be good again—better, even. However, this is only to throw you off your game, to get you to let your guard down, and as the cycles continue, they worsen each time.

A commonly observed phenomenon in abusers is splitting, or a black and white way of thinking that has no nuance. Their victim is either a perfect person or a horrible person. They are constantly labeling things in their life as good or bad, including you, and creating a confusing environment. And, speaking of confusion, you may experience a feeling of cognitive dissonance surrounding the world around you. This can affect more than just your mentality surrounding the relationship, but it can have an impact on your life with family, friends, and work. You may begin wondering if you really are remembering things wrong, and you may even think that *you* are the problem in the relationship.

Our bodies can only handle this for so long, and eventually, the trauma bond may shift into Post-Traumatic Stress Disorder (PTSD). Sadly, the only way to completely recover from a trauma bond is to go cold turkey and give up your abuser. It's important to note that just like drugs, you will have withdrawals. You will miss your abuser and it will feel painful, but following <u>the ten steps to recovery</u> will help you get through it and lead a more positive life for yourself.

If your symptoms are still severe and you're finding that your recovery is not progressing, there are placcs you can seek help as well. You don't have to do this alone, and you shouldn't! Reach out to your support, whether it be family, friends, an abuse recovery group, or even therapy. Entering therapy can help you fully understand that this was not your fault. A professional can be a great guide, helping you monitor your progress.

Remember to look back on the fictional case studies and exampes so that you can recognize the signs early on when you begin dating again. And remember, don't rush into the dating scene! It's not a competition, even though your abuser may try to make it one, flaunting a new person in your face. It will be hurtful, but don't let them upset you. They no longer have any control over your emotions or body. Remember that they will never be happy or fulfilled inside. They are not capable of true love in the same way that you are.

And, if you take one thing away from this, it should be that none of this was your fault.

You are an empathetic, kind, and forgiving person. Your abuser saw this early on and took advantage of it, but now it's *your* time to do what's best for you. Heal, rid yourself of this trauma bond, and take the path to a life free of toxic connection. You've already made tremendous progress.

How to Get Your Free Gift

To further empower you in your life journey please download:

☑ *EMPOWER YOUR LIFE - WORKBOOK*

→ **To get it scan the following QR Code**

Or go to

https://bigrocksgroup.com/recovery/

References

"20 Alarming Domestic Violence Statistics." *Social Solutions*. Accessed August 5, 2021. https://www.socialsolutions.com/blog/domestic-violence-statistics-2018/.

"39+ Subtle Signs of Trauma Bonding, Can You Relate?" *Abuse Warrior*, March 8, 2021. https://abusewarrior.com/toxic-relationships/narcissistic-abuse/signs-of-trauma-bonding/.

Fader, Sarah. "What Abusers Hope We Never Learn about Traumatic Bonding." *BetterHelp*. BetterHelp, June 12, 2017. https://www.betterhelp.com/advice/trauma/what-abusers-hope-we-never-learn-about-traumatic-bonding/.

Gilbert, Beth, Lisa Rapaport, Kim Zapata, Christina Vogt, Meryl Davids Landau, Elizabeth Millard, Becky Upham, Sarah DiGiulio, and Don Rauf. "Do You Have a CODEPENDENT Personality?" *EverydayHealth.com*. Accessed August 5, 2021. https://www.everydayhealth.com/emotional-health/do-you-have-a-codependent-personality.aspx

"Idealization and Contempt." *Psychology Today*. Sussex Publishers. Accessed August 5, 2021. https://www.psychologytoday.com/us/blog/life-after-50/201702/idealization-and-contempt.

"Identifying & Overcoming Trauma Bonds." *The Hotline*, September 22, 2020. https://www.thehotline.org/resources/trauma-bonds-what-are-they-and-how-can-we-overcome-them/.

Losey, Jennifer. "What Is a Betrayal Bond and Why Do We Stay?" *Intuitive Pathways Recovery*, January 11, 2019. https://intuitivepathwaysrecovery.com/what-is-a-betrayal-bond-and-why-do-we-stay/.

Matthew Tull, Ph.D. "Is Ptsd a Cause of Domestic Violence in Relationships?" *Verywell Mind*, January 16, 2020. https://www.verywellmind.com/ptsd-and-domestic-violence-2797405.

Matthew Tull, Ph.D. "How a Diagnosis of Complex Ptsd Differs from Ptsd." *Verywell Mind*, May 4, 2021. https://www.verywellmind.com/what-is-complex-ptsd-2797491.

Melinda. "Narcissistic Personality Disorder." *HelpGuide.org*, June 16, 2021.

https://www.helpguide.org/articles/mental-disorders/narcissistic-personality-disorder.htm.

"NCADV: National Coalition against Domestic Violence." The Nation's Leading Grassroots Voice on Domestic Violence. Accessed August 5, 2021. https://ncadv.org/STATISTICS.

Person. "Cycle of Abuse: Understanding the 4 Parts." *Healthline*. Healthline Media, November 30, 2020. https://www.healthline.com/health/relationships/cycle-of-abuse.

Person. "Trauma Bonding: What It Is and How to Cope." *Healthline*. Healthline Media, November 25, 2020. https://www.healthline.com/health/mental-health/trauma-bonding#breaking-them.

"Post-Traumatic Stress Disorder (Ptsd)." *Mayo Clinic*. Mayo Foundation for Medical Education and Research, July 6, 2018. https://www.mayoclinic.org/diseases-conditions/post-traumatic-stress-disorder/symptoms-causes/syc-20355967.

"Post-Traumatic Stress Disorder (Ptsd)." *Mayo Clinic*. Mayo Foundation for Medical Education and Research, July 6, 2018.

"Projection." *Psychology Today*. Sussex Publishers. Accessed August 5, 2021. https://www.psychologytoday.com/us/basics/projection.

Raypole, Crystal. "Betrayal Trauma: Signs and How to Start Healing." *Healthline*. Healthline Media, November 13, 2020. https://www.healthline.com/health/mental-health/betrayal-trauma.

Shahida Arabi. "Narcissists Use Trauma Bonding and Intermittent Reinforcement to Get You Addicted to Them: Why Abuse Survivors Stay." *Psych Central*. Psych Central, March 31, 2019. https://www.psychcentral.com/blog/recovering-narcissist/2019/03/narcissists-use-trauma-bonding-and-intermittent-reinforcement-to-get-you-addicted-to-them-why-abuse-survivors-stay.

Stines, Sharie. "10 Steps to Recovering from a TOXIC TRAUMA Bond." *GoodTherapy.org* Therapy Blog, August 21, 2017. https://www.goodtherapy.org/blog/10-steps-to-recovering-from-toxic-trauma-bond-0110175.

"Stockholm Syndrome and Trauma Bonding in Narcissistic Relationships." *Medium*. Psychology & Self healing, April 4, 2020. https://medium.com/psychology-self-

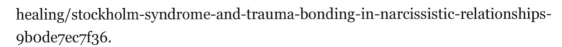

healing/stockholm-syndrome-and-trauma-bonding-in-narcissistic-relationships-9b0de7ec7f36.

"The Damage of Trauma-Bonding: How It Happens and How to Leave." *The Dawn Wellness Centre and Rehab Thailand,* July 23, 2021. https://thedawnrehab.com/blog/the-damage-of-trauma-bonding-how-it-happens-and-how-to-leave/.

"The Price and Payoff of a Gray Rock Strategy." *Psychology Today.* Sussex Publishers. Accessed August 5, 2021. https://www.psychologytoday.com/us/blog/toxic-relationships/201911/the-price-and-payoff-gray-rock-strategy.

"Trauma Bonding: Definition, Examples, Signs, and Recovery." *Medical News Today.* MediLexicon International. Accessed August 5, 2021. https://www.medicalnewstoday.com/articles/trauma-bonding#when-does-it-happen.

"What Is Gaslighting? Examples and How to Respond." Medical News Today. MediLexicon International. Accessed August 5, 2021. https://www.medicalnewstoday.com/articles/gaslighting.